Makers of the Middle Ages

Essays in Honor of William Calin

Richard Utz and Elizabeth Emery, Editors

Studies in Medievalism

Published by
Studies in Medievalism
Western Michigan University
Department of English
Kalamazoo, MI 49008-5331

ISBN 978-1-105-59754-1

Contents

Preface

Richard Utz and Elizabeth Emery

> It is possible [...] to envisage our twentieth century as a return to the Middle Ages, a century of medievalism when the medieval achievement can be better appreciated than at any time since Ariosto and Spenser. To the extent that our age contains partial repudiation of the notions of progress, technology, materialism, and secularism; that it embodies a return to symbolic thinking, religious anguish, myth making, and even, with film, radio, and television, to a partially oral culture; and that, in our fine arts, theatre, and narrative, we have gone beyond the striving for mimesis prevalent in the previous two or three centuries -- it is no longer, then, romanesque sculpture or the mystery plays or the Canterbury Tales which are other.
>
> For all these reasons I am convinced that, whatever our political options, we must emphasize the continuity and embrace the present with the past, for either, alone, separated like the honeysuckle vine and the hazelnut tree in Marie de France, will wither and perish.
>
> William Calin, *The Twentieth-Century Humanist Critics: From Spitzer to Frye*. Toronto: U of Toronto P, 2007 (182).

> La premiera partz ha nom exordi segon lati e vol dire commensamen, coma es la thema que hom pren per son commensamen, segon qu'om pot vezer cant us savis homs vol parlar solempnialmen d'alcun fag, pregan, supplican, requeren, mandan, enduzen, acosselhan o amonestan, que pren per sa thema et per son comensamen alcuna auctoritat de la Santa Escriptura o de dreg canonic, o civil, o alcun essenhamen o dig d'alcun savi o d'alqun philozophe autencticatz.
>
> Guilhem Molinier, *Las Leys d'amors*. Ed. Joseph Anglade. 4 vols. Toulouse: Edouard Privat, 1919-1920 (1 : 121).

Other scholars may fashion their praise of William Calin in voluminous *Festschriften* celebrating his impressive achievements in the study of medieval French literature, French poetry, Breton, Scots, and Occitan Studies, humanist critical traditions, and Franco-British literary relations. But for those of us laboring in the vineyard of medievalism, this *cahier* is our way of expressing gratitude for his accompanying and helping shape the study of the continuing reception of medievalia in postmedieval times. An internationally recognized Maker of the Middle Ages himself, we would like to praise Bill for inspiring us during many a conference as well as on the pages of *Studies in Medievalism* and *The Year's Work in Medievalism*. His erudition, brilliant insights, able mentoring, and wonderful sense of humor have enriched us all. This book, a compilation of brief *essais* on artists, scholars, and writers who also played a role in constructing various visions of medieval culture through the ages, is our way of extending a heartfelt *gramercy* to a friend, colleague, and fellow humanist, on the occasion of his seventy-fifth birthday.

Erasmus, Calin, Reading and Living

Jesse Swan

Of William Calin's many important contributions to knowledge and medievalisms, the extended and elaborate rumination on humanism, as Calin puts it in the title of his book, *The Twentieth-Century Humanist Critics*, provides a very nice exemplum and parable about how books, modern or even postmodern as they may be, endure and, through readers, such as Calin and those he has taught to read, how the authors of the books and their cultures, such as that represented by the *Song of Roland*, live (183-84). This is a very nicely Erasmian, participative and chiastic sentiment and way of knowing, a way of knowing that is, naturally, humanistic, but expansively humanistic, so that it acknowledges and can even celebrate its genetic and symbiotic relationship with medievalism. Like Calin, the humanist *par excellence*, Desiderius Erasmus, lives and reads and writes in ways that express himself and reflect his readers, so that his readers are at least as responsible for what they read, what they understand, as he is for what he writes, what he understands.

Aetatis suae 40, Erasmus composed his most popular, which is to say, his least unknown poem, variously titled, with the title as represented by the first print witness being, as translated by Clarence H. Miller, "Poem to Guillaume Cop, most learned of physicians, by Erasmus of Rotterdam, doctor of sacred theology, on the stealthy approach of old age and on the need to dedicate the remaining time of life to Christ, to whom we owe everything" (unless of common knowledge or otherwise indicated, poems and information on poems of Erasmus are take from Erasmus, *Collected Works*). While some, particularly in the twentieth century, have seen the poem as representing a genuine and rousing turn from a slumbering life of pleasures, Romantic readers before and liberal readers after have seen the poem as suggestive of the characteristic Erasmian turns and crosses and, perhaps to use a discourse of Erasmus's mind, holy snares. As a poem that ensnares, it is quarantined from or resisted by the reader who proceeds exclusively systematically, since that reader fails to be ensnared, fails to experience the fullness of that ecstasy Erasmus says he most reveres and seeks:

> Now I am firmly resolved, with all
> the dedication of my heart and soul, to have
> time only for Christ. . . . as
> through him I have shining and flourishing
> within me a pure mind and a sinless
> conscience, until the last day renews both body
> and mind and makes them live together as
> intimately as they once did long ago, so that
> thenceforth both parts together will enjoy a
> perpetual springtime, (Erasmus, *Collected Works*, Poem 2, ll. 229-30, 237-41)

or, more famously,

> no fools seem more senseless than those people who have been completely taken up, once and for all, with a burning devotion to Christian piety: they throw away their possessions, ignore injuries, allow themselves to be deceived, make no distinction between friend and foe, shudder at the thought of pleasure, find satisfaction in fasts, vigils, tears, and labors, shrink from life, desire death above all else — in short, they seem completely devoid of normal human responses, just as if their minds were living somewhere else, not in their bodies. Can such a condition be called anything but insanity? (Erasmus, *The Praise of Folly*, 132)

Of course, such a condition can be called something other than insanity, as any Medieval or Reformed or early modern Christian reader well knows. It can be called ecstasy. If not from common knowledge, then from the etymological note for ecstasy in the *OED*, which is exactly *apropos* Erasmus's playful amphiboly with the Christian and humanist sense of ecstasy, we can learn that in Greek, "the classical senses are 'insanity' and 'bewilderment'; but in late Gr. the etymological meaning received another application, viz., 'withdrawal of the soul from the body, mystic or prophetic trance.'" Erasmus, at 40, commits to changing his life entirely, in his poem to his lover, which is to say his ardent friend, the medical doctor, Guillaume, by committing to leave Guillaume's ecstasies for the better ecstasies of the proper theological doctor.

This is a typical Erasmian twist, as it were, with "this" referring both to the twists of he who expresses and inscribes and of she who deciphers and experiences. Whatever else Erasmus may be admired for, creating Erasmian readers, that is, readers capable of comprehending "this," is of singular importance to a culture that reveres humanity, even of and for those born poor and reared impecuniously, such as Erasmus, the illegitimate boy from Rotterdam. As Calin puts it as he ruminates on the contemporary moment of the time he inscribes his book on twentieth-century humanist critics,

> Yes, so many of the young, the gifted young — our students and our children — are held captive by their computers, television, video games, contact sports, what they call music, and their unique, never seen before, eternally riveting love life. We are not Lancelot. We cannot free them. Yet, for most of them and most of us, for all of us who come from the lower classes, however defined — everyone does sooner or later — this is the first time in history that we can benefit from culture, that the books, art, and music are ours. After all, in the golden age — say, the twelfth century — how many people were literate: two percent? five percent? At the lowest ebb of Western civilization, in the midst of barbarian invasions and all-but-total anarchy — say the seventh century — how many people were literate: one percent? Many more than one percent of our young are culturally literate. They read, they major in humanities, they tell me I am not the last dinosaur. We survived back then. We will survive now. (182-83)

Literacy, that writing that is reading that is both and never one or the other, buoys Calin as it moves all humane existence, at least as it moves "Western civilization." Riding such ebbs and flows, Erasmus teaches us, as all the humanists do. And they teach us, as Calin does, not unlike Erasmus, to participate in the insistently unstable but no less real and knowable realm of existence, even when such participation is grotesquely foolish, in many ways. As another humanist and good friend of Erasmus puts it at the opening of his great book, I will put it here, at the end of my *essai*:

> That in this shyp the chefe place I gouerne
> By this wyde see with folys wanderynge
> The cause is playne, and easy to dyscerne
> Styll am I besy bokes assemblynge
> For to haue plenty it is a plesaunt thynge
> In my conceyt and to haue them ay in honde
> But what they mene do I nat vnderstonde. (Brandt; and see poem 54 for Erasmus's epigram in honor of Brandt, an epigram that could well be made in reference to Erasmus as much as to Calin)

Bibliography

Calin, William. *The Twentieth-Century Humanist Critics: From Spitzer to Frye*. Toronto: U of Toronto P, 2007.

Brandt, Sebastian. *The Ship of Fools*. Trans. Alexander Barclay. 1509. [http://www.gutenberg.org/files/20179/20179-h/20179-h.htm#p017]. Accessed 4 February 2011.

Erasmus of Rotterdam. *The Praise of Folly*. Trans. & ed. Clarence H. Miller. New Haven: Yale UP, 1979.

Erasmus of Rotterdam. *Collected Works of Erasmus: Poems*. Vols. 85 & 86. Trans. Clarence H. Miller, ed. & ann. Harry Vredeveld. Toronto: U of Toronto P, 1993.

Madame de Sévigné's Aristocratic Medievalism

Alicia C. Montoya

In the vast picture of darkness that is the *Grand Siècle*'s rejection of everything medieval, a lone beacon of light is offered by Madame de Sévigné's radiant medievalism. For Marie de Rabutin-Chantal, marquise de Sévigné, did not merely love the medieval: she lived it and embodied it, in every sense of the word. "Going medieval" was for her not a conscious choice or—as we would have it today—a life-style, but her very identity. In this sense, her medievalism was part of a distinctly aristocratic engagement with the Middle Ages that was eclipsed by the end of the Ancien Régime and the break with the feudal past brought about by the French Revolution.

Madame de Sévigné was a full-blooded aristocrat, and as an aristocrat, she viewed the medieval in personal, familial, or even proprietary terms. The Middle Ages were a defining element of every aristocrat's genealogical identity. Belonging to the ancient nobility—as opposed to the more recent *noblesse de robe* created by Louis XIV—rested on family histories that went back to a medieval, chivalrous past. But under Louis XIV, the aristocracy underwent an identity crisis, as the Sun King pulled everyone and everything into his own orbit, depriving families such as Sévigné's of their ancient prerogatives. The blinding light of the King ushered in a period of darkness for the nobility, who instead turned to the Middle Ages as their own source of light, a lost Golden Age to contrast to modern degeneration.

The hundreds of letters—by turns witty, literate, gossipy, passionate, contemplative—that Madame de Sévigné wrote from the 1670s through 1690s bear witness to this aristocratic turn to the Middle Ages. Called upon by Louis XIV to provide proofs of their nobility, members of the old aristocracy developed a new interest in medieval charters, genealogies, and chivalric orders. In her letters, Sévigné obsessed about her family genealogy, as well as that of the illustrious family her daughter had married into, the ancient Provençal house of Adhémar. Among her earliest writings are a series of exchanges with her profligate cousin Roger de Bussy-Rabutin on the family genealogy he was compiling, that established their ascendance back to a mythical founding ancestor in 1118. Critically eyeing her contemporaries' claims to nobility, Sévigné revealed an astoundingly long historical memory, proving the existence in the seventeenth century of that supremely French notion, the *longue durée*. Speaking in one letter of a common acquaintance, a magistrate, she casually noted, as if she had been there herself, that "he was already a nobleman" when he received his position as a reward from Philip Augustus—i.e., in the twelfth century!

For Madame de Sévigné, the key notion when speaking of her family history was that of chivalry, and she regularly spoke of "*notre* belle et ancienne chevalerie." This common sense of chivalry united all aristocratic families. Knowing one's own medieval genealogy, and its historic links to chivalry, enabled aristocrats like Sévigné to know who they *really* were. There is a very real feeling in her letters that the medieval reveals deeper truths, both in a historical and in a moral sense.

For there are also important links between *chevalerie* and *noblesse,* which is a moral concept. To be an aristocrat meant, in the most basic sense, to behave medievally. And conversely, being medieval meant, too, behaving aristocratically or like a "noble." The word "aristocrat," of course, is a later, Revolutionary invention. In the seventeenth century, the only term that existed to designate an aristocrat was "noble." Playing the role of mother-in-law with gusto, Madame de Sévigné rebukes her son-in-law for sullying the blood of the Adhémar family by his unchivalrous behavior toward her daughter. To make her point clear, she reminds him of a Crusader ancestor, some six hundred years ago, who would be turning in his grave at his descendant's present actions. (Not surprisingly, there has been some speculation about why her daughter and son-in-law chose to move 400 miles away from Paris, where she remained living, and why all her daughter's replies mysteriously dis-appeared.)

But there is more to Madame de Sévigné's medievalism than seventeenth-century aristocratic identity politics. The Middle Ages are not only a kind of family business; they are also the stuff of family romance, for her medievalness explains Madame de Sévigné's own literary profusions. In the letters, the medieval, crucially, evokes the *romanesque*—the term that in the eighteenth century, from being a synonym, evolved into our modern *romantique* or romantic. When she reads Maimbourg's *Croisades,* Madame de Sévigné dreams of her daughter's family ancestors, who are really described in the book—both Aimar de Monteil and a member of the Castellane family figure in it. Maimbourg's historical *Croisades* in turn remind her of Tasso's fictional chivalric epic *Gerusalemme Liberata*. Tasso, too, describes the deeds of historical Crusader figures who were, in fact, real ancestors of the Grignan family.

Madame de Sévigné lives her life like a romance and it is a medieval *roman,* not a modern one. When writing to Bussy-Rabutin, she refers to her daughter not by her name, but as "la belle Madelonne," the eponymous heroine of the fifteenth-century *Histoire de Pierre de Provence et la belle Maguelonne*. Her lapdog is called Marphise, after a character in Ariosto's *Orlando Furioso*. Her daughter's chateau in Grignan she calls the "château d'Apollidon," after the wondrous castle in the chivalric romance *Amadis de Gaule*. Wandering in the woods around her estate, she carves verses into the trees, in imitation of the love-lorn characters in Ariosto. The medieval, in other words, is like the air she breathes, it is the timeframe in which she lives her daily life.

To complete the picture, there are the literary forebears. Madame de Sévigné is quite taken with the story of one Guillaume Adhémar, whose mistress was supposedly the well-known *trobairitz* comtesse de Die. Never mind that the biography Madame de Sévigné read of Guillaume Adhémar was a romanticized, not to say spurious account written by Nostra-damus' lesser-known brother, Jean de Nostredame. What matters is that, in Madame de Sévigné's eyes, literature and the medieval touch one another so perfectly. To be medieval was to fantasize, and even—like Tasso and Ariosto, like Guillaume Adhémar and the comtesse de Die—to write.

The ultimate proof of Madame de Sévigné's medievalism is, finally, in her endless stream of letters, a textual chain linking the medieval past to the present. There is perhaps no better recognition of this than a curious poem that the society journal *Mercure de France*, getting wind of her letters, published in 1690. In this poem, "from the troubadour Adhémar to the countess of Grignan," a voice from the medieval past literally speaks with the present, incarnated in Madame de Sévigné's daughter. When the poem's opening lines refer to "a famous troubadour who has left his dark abode for you," one can ask how we should read the allusion to darkness. For the darkness is not that of the troubadour's Middle Ages. The darkness was that of the present day, in which the long shadow cast by Louis left so little space for the medieval to shine through.

Bibliography

Sévigné, Madame de. *Correspondance*. 3 vols. Ed. Roger Duchêne. Paris: Gallimard, 1972-78.

Montoya, Alicia. "Naturalizing the Commonplace. Two Readings of Tasso during the Long Eighteenth Century (Sévigné, Rousseau)." In: J.W. Koopmans and N.H. Petersen (eds.), *Commonplace Culture in Western Europe in the Early Modern Period*. Vol. III: *Legitimation of Authority*. Leuven: Peeters, 2011. 75-96.

Pound's Troubadours

Willam D. Paden

Ezra Pound knew the troubadours well, having studied them as an undergraduate at Hamilton College in Spring 1905 and as a graduate student at the University of Pennsylvania in 1905-1907. Realizing his calling to become a poet with scholarly horizons, not a scholar, he relocated to London, then Paris, and eventually Italy, but never ceased to find inspiration in the troubadours. He wrote in their defense, "The mirth of Provençal song is at times anything but sunburnt, and the mood is often anything but idle" (*LE* 94), arguing with Keats, who in his "Ode on a Grecian Urn" had expressed yearning for "Provençal song, and sunburnt mirth." Other poets including Browning, Swinburne, Carducci, and Rostand had invoked the troubadours as singers of love, especially the distant love of Jaufre Rudel, an ethereal passion that had little appeal for Pound. His remark about sunburn and idleness was unfair to his predecessors since his favorite, Bertran de Born, had appeared—as a tragic lover, it is true—in a lengthy narrative poem by Eleanor Anne Porden (*Coeur de Lion,* 1822), again as a war poet in the classical mould (Victor Pierre Laurens, *Le Tyrtée du Moyen Âge*, 1863), and in a novel by Maurice Hewlett (*The Life and Death of Richard Yea-and-Nay*, 1900), who later became Pound's friend. Sordello, another favorite, had appeared as an alter ego in Browning's *Sordello* (1840). Reading this poem gave Pound his first stimulus to learn Provençal. Within a year he began to study the language, and he published his first translation ("Alba Belingalis") in 1905, while still an undergraduate.

In erudition Pound far surpassed these predecessors. In his poems, translations, and essays he named nearly fifty troubadours great and small of the 360-odd whose names survive. He relied on an intervening source, the thirteenth-century prose vidas ("lives" of the poets) and razos ("reasons" for the composition of a song). In his essay "Troubadours: Their Sorts and Conditions" and elsewhere he referred to vidas and razos for most of the Provençal poets he mentioned, showing knowledge of a third of the extant prose texts. For quite a few minor figures he referred to the prose pieces but no songs. Two of his poems, "Marvoil" and "Piere Vidal Old," versify stories from razos. He alluded repeatedly to the adventure-packed vida of Sordello, while mentioning three of his songs just once. His access to the troubadours was facilitated by the prose pieces, which are easier to read than the poetry. Although they are unreliable as history, especially as love stories, they provided the poet with the mythic view that he sought.

Nevertheless he cited some eighty troubadour poems. He focused on the great figures of the twelfth century, foremost Arnaut Daniel and Bertran de Born, but also Bernart de Ventadorn, Giraut de Bornelh, and others. He translated Arnaut in 1910 and mentioned him as late as 1960 (*Canto CX*). He was as obsessive about Arnaut's contemporary Bertran de Born, whose "War Song" occupied him from 1910, when he translated it in *The Spirit of Romance,* through 1959 (*Canto CV*). In "Troubadours: Their Sorts and Conditions" he extended his remarks into the thirteenth century, dwelling on the satirist Peire Cardenal. For Peire, unlike Arnaut and Bertran, no individual edition existed; indeed Peire's songs had never been published with a translation. The lack of a helpful edition shows. Pound's versions are mostly reasonable, but one is botched. "Ready for war, as night is to follow the sun" (*LE* 107) is Pound's misunderstanding of a line that means quite literally, "He has war nearby who has it on his land." Pound did no better with the rest of the stanza.

In "Near Perigord" Pound has Arnaut Daniel perform a song by his friend Bertran de Born, and Arnaut adds that he "Envies its vigor . . . and deplores the technique" (*PT* 306). Bertran's vigor drew Pound. In "Sestina: Altaforte" Pound's imagination ran riot: apparently afflicted with lycanthropy, Bertran cries out that when the battlefield runs red with blood, "Then howl I my heart nigh mad with rejoicing." This excess distorts the warlike temper of the historical troubadour. Pound also looked to Bertran for vigor in love and found it in his song about the imaginary lady, which he translated ("Dompna Pois De Me No'us Cal"), used for a rumination on memory ("Provincia Deserta"), and took as the point of departure for "Na Audiart." In the source Bertran begs his lady's permission, since she will not love him, to invent and love an imaginary lady compounded of the best features of beauties from miles around. In "Na Audiart" Pound begins with Bertran's address to one of these, asking her to lend him her delightful shape, and turns it into a plea to grant her love now when she is young. The argument recalls Herrick's "Gather ye rosebuds while ye may," a humanistic conceit that differs deeply from Bertran's poem; but Pound gives his version a lovely lilting rhythm. In "Near Perigord" he attempts to demystify what he called "chivalric love," reasoning that Bertran's poem about these ladies is really about their castles, not a love poem but a political one. He depicts Bertran with a red beard and green eyes, which were his own colors. He projected himself into the troubadour.

For technique Pound's admiration of Arnaut Daniel was unbounded. He did not use Arnaut's work in original compositions, as he did Bertran's, nor was he greatly interested in Arnaut's role in the vidas, as he was for other troubadours. But he translated sixteen of Arnaut's eighteen songs. In his most successful efforts he managed to say what Arnaut had said, to do it in stanzas rhyming in the same patterns, and to employ rhymes using the same sounds in the two languages. These tours de force show the hand of a poet of extraordinary skill, a wizard capable of making modern English say and sound the same as medieval Provençal. Diction, however, is another matter. Drawing on medieval Scots, Pound tricked out his Arnaut with archaic words that have no correspondence in the original. Pound's "galzeardy," for example (*PT* 521), is a Scots spelling for archaic "galliardise" (the z represents the letter yogh, pronounced as y). But in Pound's version of Arnaut it corresponds to Provençal "deport," which means the same ("gaiety, mirth, revelry") but is neither archaic nor dialectal. For the troubadours "deport" was a plain word. By adorning his versions of Arnaut with such archaisms, Pound replicated the experience not of the medieval Provençal audience but of the modern student – that is Pound himself. His self-consciousness got in the way of his translation.

In his wake came other poets who have continued his interest. They have rarely engaged the troubadours in original work, but have shown an appetite to translate their Provençal. For their awareness of medieval poetry, and that of their readers, Pound deserves thanks. Several have gone beyond him in attempting to create singable translations, which is ironic since he professed exactly such a desire although his work rarely shows it. ("Na Audiart" may come closest.) Of the troubadours Pound might have said, as he did say in *Canto CXVI*, "I cannot make it cohere."

Bibliography

Makin, Peter. *Provence and Pound*. Berkeley: U of California P, 1978.

Paden, William D. "Provençal and the Troubadours." *Ezra Pound in Context*. Ed. Ira B. Nadel. Cambridge: Cambridge UP, 2010. Pp. 181-91.

Pound, Ezra. *The Cantos*. New York: New Directions, 1993.

---. *Literary Essays*. Edited with an introduction by T.S. Eliot. London: Faber and Faber, 1968.

---. *Poems and Translations*. Ed. Richard Sieburth. New York: Library of America, 2003.

---. *The Spirit of Romance*. New York: New Directions, 1968.

Rosenstein, Roy S. "Translation." *A Handbook of the Troubadours*. Ed. F.R.P. Akehurst and Judith M. Davis. Berkeley: U of California P, 1995. Pp. 334-48.

Helen Waddell at Columbia: Maker of Medievalists

Roy Rosenstein

Including Helen Waddell (1889-1965) among key figures in Medieval Studies suggests that the spirit of H.W. (as she signed correspondence) may be returning from a long exile. She previously figured only in *Women Medievalists and the Academy*. And before that, academics relied on P.G. Walsh's obituary notice. Helen Waddell was a name murmured passionately by future medievalists outside the classroom but was usually absent from their professors' reading lists. She seemed a brief candle outshined by a galaxy of brighter luminaries. Yet her radiance and warmth remain undimmed despite neglect and disparagement. Perhaps her zenith has finally been reached and her brilliance will at last be recognized. Helen Waddell is better remembered now than C.H. Haskins or G.G. Coulton. Those two makers of the Middle Ages—one praised her to the skies, the other blocked her rising star—both predeceased her and receive scant tribute today.

H.W.'s importance has been understated even at Columbia, where in 1935 she received her only American honorary doctorate, from Nicholas Murray Butler. By the 1970s, on campus Waddell commanded effusive loyalty along with dismissive criticism. W.T.H. Jackson ranked her work as "popular but overly romanticized" while elsewhere in Philosophy Hall another Latinist, Dan Penham, endorsed her translations only. In 1927, her mentor George Saintsbury had anticipated this disagreement over his *princesse lointaine*'s work: "Anyone who fails to enjoy it—scholar or general reader—is profoundly to be pitied." Her influence has nevertheless been widespread and enduring. She may have inspired more medievalists than Pound, who brought Jim Wilhelm and George Wolf to Arnaut Daniel. I encountered the troubadours through H.W. Not a maker of the Middle Ages, she made medievalists. Yet Waddell, like fellow poet-translator Sally Purcell, held no academic appointment. Her comet-like career was short: a self-sacrificing attention to her step-mother until 1920, a gray-haired resumption of her studies, a premature curtailment following WWII shell shock. Between 1927 and 1947, her writings united criticism, fiction, and translation in the heady realm of literature.

Richard Katz reminded students how many French Renaissance poets are forgotten because they did not write in French. How plentiful then were the resurrected medieval Latin writers in *The Wandering Scholars,* both a page-turner and eye-opener. Through her overview we met Salimbene, until then Coulton's *chasse gardée*. Giraldus Cambrensis, as known to her readers, is now in Penguin as Gerald of Wales. In thumbnail portraits of these and others, Waddell brought medieval writers to life as Auerbach, Curtius, or Spitzer did not. If those academics are indispensable for the broad synthesis or a close analysis, the individual writers sparkle under H.W.'s pen even when she cites the dreary *Patrologia*: early in her studies she read all 217 volumes! With her Latin training she did not need Migne's 1866 companion *Lexicon,* which I consulted in what had been Gilbert Highet's copy. How else to interpret *trutannus et trufator,* post-classical epithets characterizing Primas and Archipoeta, on whom I would eventually write a dissertation chapter. Hers is a world aswarm with striking characters and world-class poets: presented, cited, translated, although never enough of the last for the Latin novices we were. Her cameo portraits introduced dear friends as though they were her contemporaries, so intimately did she frequent them. With a well-turned translation she painted a fellow poet. Hildebert's "Lost the eternal April, for the sake of a passing spring!" encapsulated an entire world. Her *Peter Abelard: A Novel* triumphed from its first pages, where he scribbles in the margins of his Latin manuscript a translation of the French song outside his window: "Temps s'en vait et rien n'ai fait, temps s'en vient et ne fais rien." Decades later, I discovered those Latin marginalia exist: "Fugit hora, absque mora, nihil facio." H.W. invested history in her story of a solitary philosopher distracted from the eternal April by a passing rhyme, then by his prize student. Centuries later, another Parisian philosopher abandoned his classroom for a co-ed. Had he been teaching her Abelard? Had he too read the novel which was translated into French and eight more languages?

Waddell was herself born to translate, from Latin and French. When Donald Frame revised his version of *Manon Lescaut*, he wrote me how among those previously available he "liked best Helen Waddell's." H.W. interpreted not so much others' ideas as she did the language they wrote. When she projects herself onto Abelard, writing with E.K. Rand's fondness for Jerome, patron saint to translators, she portrays Abelard as a fellow interpreter. Contrary to Hildebert, she imagined the loss of an afterlife recompensed in earthly joys like those shared by Heloise and Abelard satisfying their passion on the altar. That experience of joy, central to Hildebert's warning, was erotically charged for vernacular *vagans* Jaufre Rudel. In a graduate class I took as an undergraduate, H.W.'s version of "Lanquan li jorn" was cited as the best ever of his May song. Later in print I would stray from that appraisal, but in 1971 it propelled me to Ideal Bookstore on Amsterdam and 116th. The published translation differs from the signed holograph I found forty years later tipped into her first book, *Lyrics from the Chinese*, recommended by sinologists from Lin Yutang to Arthur Cooper. H.W. practiced *mouvance* in revising and circulating her translation. But the London reprint in which I first read the published version has never left this wandering scholar's library. Like other admiring readers, I now buy up old Anchor paperback copies to give to medievalist students.

H.W.'s Middle Ages—panoramic yet poetic, factual but inspired—was inspirational. While my classmates followed Huizinga, whose work would frame my dissertation, I pursued H.W., deceased six years before. Like Poe's Helen, she represented the distant shore, the Ithaka I sought, not classical Greece but the Latin Middle Ages. She knew the loyalty her writings aroused when, the toast of Thirties London, opting against husband or children, she preferred readers "who belong to me, and are bound to feel a little in love." Was it a jealous lover's complaint when V.S. Pritchett mourned her *Wandering Scholars*, "pinched" from his library?

In her 1947 W.P. Ker lecture, before the darkness of Alzheimer's shut H.W. off from the world, she eulogized Ker and praised his *Dark Ages* as "a small book but with the quality of radium," recounting how he led her to discover Boethius. Today a small readership admires the white heat of her books as we are drawn to the period, figures, and lyrics she so enticingly introduces. *The Wandering Scholars* is unlike Remy de Gourmont's *Latin mystique*, which boasted two noted readers, Huysmans and his Des Esseintes. H.W. may no longer have as many as she merits, but she has won more than a happy few to Medieval Latin poetry.

I write these prosaic lines as the 2011 Roy Fellow at the University of South Carolina, dividing my day between Rare Books and main library. The former preserves H.W.'s limited-edition titles while the stacks boast three or four circulating copies each of *The Wandering Scholars* and *Medieval Latin Lyrics*. By them on the shelves is the latest book on Venantius Fortunatus, one of H.W.'s favorites with five poems in her anthology. The study cites Alan Cameron on Egyptian wandering scholars, then references European *vagantes* in the index. Helen Waddell, who coined their English label and gave them new life, is missing from the book's bibliography.

Bibliography

Blackett, Monica. *The Mark of the Maker: A Portrait of Helen Waddell*. London: Constable, 1973.

Corrigan, D. Felicitas. *Helen Waddell: A Biography*. London: Gollancz, 1990.

FitzGerald, Jennifer. "Helen Waddell...." *Women Medievalists and the Academy*, ed. Jane Chance. Madison, WI: University of Wisconsin P, 2005. Pp. 322-38.

Gilbank, Robin. "Helen Waddell....." Handbook of Medieval

Studies. Ed. Albrecht Classen. Berlin: De Gruyter, 2010. In the section on "Key Figures." Vol. 3: 2702-05.

Harrington, Susan T. "Helen Waddell." *Late Nineteenth-Century and Early Twentieth-Century British Women Poets*, ed. William B. Thesing. Detroit: Gale, 2001. Pp. 293-98.

Waddell, Helen. *The Wandering Scholars*, 1927.

---. *Medieval Latin Lyrics*, 1929.

---. *Peter Abelard: A Novel*, 1933.

---. *Poetry in the Dark Ages*, 1948.

---. *More Latin Lyrics*, 1976.

---. *Songs of the Wandering Scholars*, 1982.

Walsh, P.G. "Waddell, Helen Jane." *Dictionary of National Biography* 56 (2004): 637-39.

Jaufre Rudel.

When the days lengthen in the month of May
Well pleased am I to hear the birds
Sing far away
But when from that place I am gone
I hang my head and make dull moan
Since she my life is set upon
Is far away

So far that song of bird, flower of the thorn,
Please me no more than winter morn
With ice and sleet.
Ah would I were a pilgrim overseas
With staff and scrip and cloak to cover me
That someday I might kneel me on one knee
Before her feet.

Most sad, most joyous shall I go away
Let me have seen her for a single day
My love afar.
I shall not see her: for her land and mine
Are sundered and the ways are hard to find,
So many ways, and I shall lose my way;
So wills it God

Yet shall I know no other love but her,
And if not her no other love at all.
She hath surpassed all.
So fair she is, so noble, I would be
A captive with the hosts of paynimrie
In a far land, if so ~~that~~ be upon me
Her eyes might fall.

God who hath made all things on earth that are,
That made my love, and set her thus afar,
Grant me this grace
That some day I may come within a room
Or in some garden gloom
Look on her face.

It will not be, for at my birth they said
That one had put this doom upon my head
— God curse him among men
That I should love, and not till I ~~be~~ dead
Be loved again.

H W.

Seamus Heaney and Beowulf

M.J. Toswell

Anglo-Saxonists everywhere should celebrate, perhaps annually in a brief offering of gifts at a local temple, the remarkable fact that Seamus Heaney completed his commissioned translation of *Beowulf* and published it in 1999, creating the first breaking wave of what was already a gradual tidal swell of interest in the text. Perhaps they should also celebrate the decision of that year's Whitbread panel, which came down to the vote of the Texan model Jerry Hall, who famously decided that Heaney's *Beowulf* offered more to posterity than the first Harry Potter novel and awarded him the prize. As a recent Nobel prizewinner, Heaney brought the star factor to publication of a new translation of a 3182-line poem surviving in a manuscript written nearly a thousand years earlier. The idiosyncracies of his work remain deservedly ignored in the oceanic surge of gratitude that we should pour out upon him. That breaking wave turned out to be the one the surfers call the avalanche, the biggest wave of the set. The following waves, a plethora of movies, graphic novels, and even the odd opera, might qualify as corduroy, the surfer term for a series of waves coming in close formation.

But in retrospect, the Heaney version of *Beowulf* was the monster wave coming after very few harbinger waves, an unexpected avalanche, the best break of the series. And yet, the idiosyncracies of *Heaneywulf*, as it is often termed, niggle at us. Heaney himself describes the register of his translation as evoking his uncles in northern Ireland, with their slow, somewhat methodical and deep-voiced statements about life on the farm where Heaney grew up—Mossbawn. The language of the translation is imbued with Celticisms—the hall at Heorot is a "bawn," and the warriors wear "graiths" rather than body-armour. It is a hard life, and Heaney presents it well, reaching for stately grandeur in the speeches of the characters, melodrama during the encounters with the creatures who harry the lives of the Geats and Danes, and elegant but precise exposition of the source text through most of the poem. Heaney uses a flexible tetrameter line with alliteration, evoking the Old English poetic style without being hampered by its details. The language is heightened, with extra caesuras to mark the syntax as somewhat archaic; thus the poet depicts the ship that awaits Scyld Scefing at the beginning of the poem: "A ring-whorled prow rode in the harbour,/ice-clad, outbound, a craft for a prince." The translation is literal and nostalgic, accurate and evocative.

The life of an ordinary translator is a difficult one, involving the effort to efface oneself in producing a text that evokes the original author wholly, channelling only what the author might have written if expert in the target language. The life of a famous translator is strikingly different, because such a translator can rework the text, making it anew and establishing a new standard for the present day. Thus in the mid-twentieth century Nevill Coghill's translation of Chaucer's *Canterbury Tales* was almost better-known than the original text, as was Chapman's translation of Homer in Keats's day (a comparison frequently adduced in reviews of Heaney's work), and just as Heaney's version of *Beowulf* is fated to be better-known in the early twenty-first century than the original. Moreover, Heaney's work has been trammelled about with the *auctoritas* of modern Anglo-Saxon scholarship. Commissioned by Norton in the early 1980s, and initially seeing the light of day as individual pieces in some of the poetry collections which earned Heaney his Nobel Prize in 1995, the *Beowulf* has been through many iterations, all of them ostensibly planned by the publishers and all of them heralded by a quite remarkable marketing machine. The translation was first published as a separate volume in English and in North America (with strikingly different covers—the European one with subdued and mysterious hints of fire on a black background, and the North American one with a martial but wholly anonymous human figure from the shoulders up covered in chainmail), then brought out in the next Norton Anthology for first-year English students to replace the venerable but rather dull E. Talbot Donaldson translation, and then produced in a facing-page Old English and Heaney version. Next, Norton emitted the translation again, this time in a full critical edition (though somewhat amazingly the Heaney text stands in for the original poem) with supplementary criticism and edited by Daniel Donoghue. Most recently, in 2007, emerged an illustrated edition with photos chosen by J.D. Niles, the current president of the International Association of Anglo-Saxonists. In other words, the Heaney translation receives the full stamp of approval, buttressed as it is by the full forces of Anglo-Saxonist critics and editors.

Of course, Heaneywulf is not Heaney's only translation; in fact, rethinking cultural determinism might be described as a Heaney passion, since before *Beowulf* there were extended translations from Ovid, two Sophocles plays, his version of the medieval Irish figure of mad Sweeney from the poem *Buile Suibhne,* and a series of Eastern European and Russian poets. After *Beowulf,* indicating that his interest in matters medieval continues, Heaney has published his take on Robert Henryson's Scottish response to Chaucer's *Troilus and Criseyde,* the *Testament of Cresseid,* again separately in a smaller edition, and later as part of his mainstream work. Heaney is also a prolific commentator on his own and other people's work, producing important statements about the role of poetry in the modern era. Having studied the traditional curriculum of English Language and Literature at the Queen's University Belfast as a young man, and taught it in various schools for some years thereafter, Heaney knows what he is about. When he claims *Beowulf* as a Celtic text, he is fully aware that he is engaging in a postcolonial reclamation project that, if carried through, would mark all English achievements as either Celtic or Viking. It is both a puckish and a deeply intellectual approach. In a more subtle way it reflects the resurgent tribalisms of the twenty-first century, as Heaney takes a poem written in Old English about events taking place in Denmark and Sweden several centuries earlier and reworks it into a consideration of sectarian conflict and tribal hatred in a markedly Irish context. His reworking of *Beowulf*, like much of his poetry, juxtaposes an apparent fidelity to the text with a mythopoeic challenge to cultural predispositions. Heaney, while rooted in northern Ireland, wants to be a world citizen and to create texts which query our preconceptions in political and ethical ways; his *Beowulf*, Heaneywulf, may not be the avalanche of this kind of textual intervention in public perception, but it is certainly a wave that surges to a remarkable crest.

Bibliography

Crowder, Ashby Bland, and Jason David Hall, eds. *Seamus Heaney: Poet, Critic, Translator*. Basingstoke: Palgrave, 2007.

Heaney, Seamus, trans. *Beowulf*. London: Faber & Faber, 1999.

McCarthy, Conor. *Seamus Heaney and Medieval Poetry*. Woodbridge: D.S. Brewer, 2008.

Milfull, Inge and Hans Sauer, "Seamus Heaney: Ulster, Old English, and *Beowulf*," in *Bookmarks from the Past: Studies in Early English Language and Literature in Honour of Helmut Gneuss*. Eds. Lucia Kornexl and Ursula Lenker. Frankfurt: Lang, 2003. Pp. 81-141.

O'Donoghue, Bernard. *The Cambridge Companion to Seamus Heaney*. Cambridge: Cambridge UP, 2009.

Vendler, Helen. *Seamus Heaney*. Cambridge, MA: Harvard UP, 1998.

Rudyard Kipling

Tom Shippey

Only nine of Kipling's more than 250 published stories are set in the Middle Ages, and he rarely shows deeper knowledge of the period than could be gained from popular sources, like the Keary sisters' 1891 *Heroes of Asgard*, mentioned by Una in *Puck of Pook's Hill*, or the Longfellow poems quoted or alluded to several times. Despite that, Kipling's images of the Middle Ages have sometimes proved surprisingly productive; and when they were not, they may still seem prophetic—even if this prophet has, once again, found no honor in his own country.

Kipling's greatest contribution to later fictions on the Middle Ages comes from one of his five "Roman" stories, three of which form a connected sequence in *Puck of Pook's Hill* (1906). The critical moment comes when the girl Una asks the centurion Parnesius (who has just called Romans fools), "But you're a Roman yourself, aren't you?" With his hooped armor, oblong shield, and red-crested helmet, Parnesius would seem unmistakably Roman, but he answers, "Ye-es and no." What he means is that while he is Roman by birth, language, and culture, he is British-born. And what Kipling means (as was certainly clearer in 1906 than a century later) is that the Roman Empire had close parallels with the British Empire, and that in both cases the true Romans, or Britons, were not the stay-at-homes but those, often born abroad of parents born abroad, who guarded the frontiers, ruled the provinces, settled the colonies—the "Outside Men," as Kipling sometimes called them. The parallel was to become a staple of twentieth-century Arthurian fiction, often produced by writers from service families or with imperial connections.

Kipling's more definitively medieval sequence is also to be found in *Puck of Pook's Hill*, four stories centered on Hugh the Saxon and Sir Richard the Norman, with a coda involving them in the 1910 "Puck" sequel *Rewards and Fairies* ("The Tree of Justice"), and another coda dealing with the fate of their treasure in *Puck* itself ("The Treasure and the Law"). These pick up a theme which had been familiar since the time of Sir Walter Scott. It is a variant of the American "melting-pot" myth, and insists above all that the term "English" has no meaning *per se* but only as indicator of a coalescence, itself merged into the later coalescence, "British." The theory is put forward in narrative terms by Hugh the Saxon and Richard the Norman becoming friends, and then brothers-in-law, after fighting each other at Hastings, but is overtly stated by the Norman overlord De Aquila, who is guarding Pevensey on the south coast against a second invasion from Normandy: "I am not Norman, Sir Richard, nor Saxon, Sir Hugh. English am I."

Centurion Parnesius had come to the same conclusion, in a sense, when he refused imperial promotion and opted to stay on Hadrian's Wall, guarding the north of England as De Aquila guards the south. Parnesius further shows signs of fellow-feeling with the Picts beyond the Wall (representing the Scots, in Kipling's time enthusiastic partners in the British Empire), as well as the "Winged Hats" who attack it. These seem iconographically (if anachronistically) to be Danes, and so represent another known part of the pre-modern English ethnic mix. Roman, Dane, Saxon, Norman: for Kipling, as for Scott, for modern British politicians, and academics as well, "English" has no meaning other than "all the above." The recipient of these words will be aware that some few have ventured to reject the thesis, as politically motivated—but very few; and it is not surprising that Kipling's scenes continue to be replayed in modern form, as for instance "The Tree of Justice" is in George Shipway's 1969 novel *Knight in Anarchy*, or Julian Rathbone's 1997 *The Last English King*. They fit modern preoccupations too well to be let die.

This has not been the case with all of Kipling's "medieval" and "Roman" stories. In his own time Kipling's detached attitude to Christianity, his tolerance of pagan belief, and the way in which he suggests (with characteristic indirection) that Christ's ransoming of humanity might find admirable parallels on a human level, especially among the "Outside Men" or "children of Martha": these may then have seemed somewhat disturbing, but they have little shock-value now. Elsewhere attitudes have changed so much, especially with regard to race and class, that Kipling's nuances (and I repeat that he was a strikingly nuanced author) are simply not understood.

This is the case with one story which has attracted a little modern critical attention, "The Finest Story in the World," from the 1891 collection *Many Inventions*. In this the narrator, obviously meant to suggest Kipling himself, makes the acquaintance of a London clerk called Charlie, who has literary aspirations. These aspirations are soon revealed to be hopelessly naïve, but the narrator realises that there is more in Charlie than Charlie knows. Under certain conditions he is capable of remembering his past lives: one as a Greek galley-slave (and in his half-trance Charlie reproduces a Greek graffito of which he could have no conscious knowledge), one as a Norseman sailing with Leif Eiriksson to America (Charlie again in trance corroborating and adding to the "Vinland sagas" which by Kipling's time had become familiar).

But what is the point of the story? It has been set, by John Carey, within the context of what was in two senses a Victorian *querelle des clercs*, one between different groups of a newly-enlarged clerisy, and one concerning the status of "clerks" themselves, people like Charlie. I entirely agree with Carey's overall thesis about the alarmed reactions of the traditional literary class to a new demographic literacy. But Kipling, I am sure, was still writing for his own constituency of "the Outside Men," and they may have seen the story differently. Briefly, I would suggest that the story presents a hierarchy of narrative. At the top, the "finest story" itself is the one that never gets told, the one that would have combined Charlie's priceless first-hand knowledge with the narrator's literary skill. At the bottom are the bumbling attempts at fiction and poetry of Charlie's own conscious self. In between are the scraps he emits in trance; and, interestingly, provoking one trance, the poetry of Longfellow, himself trying to reproduce medieval narratives which he was sometimes the first to bring to general attention.

The main point I would make, though, is this. To Kipling, the medieval world is the realistic one, not the half-life "real world" of commercial London. And that medieval world has not died, but shifted "outside," to people the literary classes do not encounter: to "Regimental Bards," to the authors of "Barrack-Room Ballads," and the creators of "Tribal Lays." Kipling may value "medievalism," but he is aware also of people who re-live it—and not only, like Charlie, unconsciously.

Bibliography

Carey, John. *The Intellectuals and the Masses: Pride and Prejudice Among the Literary Intelligentsia, 1880-1939*. London: Faber & Faber, 1992.

Mackenzie, Donald. "Kipling and Northernness." *Kipling Journal* 81 (2007): 21-43.

Wawn, Andrew. "Vínland in British Literature to 1946." In: Geraldine Barnes, ed., *Viking America: the First Millennium*. Cambridge: D.S. Brewer. 2001. Pp. 191-206.

Williams, Deanne. "Rudyard Kipling and the Norman Conquest." *Ariel: A Review of International English Literature* 39.3 (2008). [http://ariel.synergiesprairies.ca/ariel/index.php/ariel/issue/view/24]. Accessed 23 January 2011.

J.R.R. Tolkien: Medievalism and Middle-Earth

Gwendolyn A. Morgan

J.R.R. Tolkien's contribution to the field of medievalism is almost a redundancy. Scholars and aficionados alike credit his tales of Middle-Earth as the source of modern fantasy, most of which also centers around such creatures as Celtic wizards and faerie, Anglo-Saxon dwarfs and gnomes, Nordic dragons, shape-shifters, and objects of magical power. Indeed, fictional Middle-Earth, which Tolkien adapted from Anglo-Saxon *middengeard* (literally, "middle-yard') has entered the vocabulary of fantasy fiction, from novel to film to video game to comic book, as a common noun. His fiction has generated cinematic versions and inspired giants of popular music as diverse as the Beatles and the Moody Blues (who can forget the Ents of "Tuesday Afternoon"?). Its influence in popular art is evinced in one's inability in the last several decades to pass a bookstore without encountering a display of, if not Tolkien calendars, certainly those featuring fairies, dragons, and elves, with posters and mass-produced art to match. Even politics reflect Tolkien's influence: some six years ago, a photograph emphasizing George W. Bush's wedding ring and bearing the caption, "Frodo is dead; Bush has the Ring," flooded over the Internet. It's not merely the joke; it's the fact that "the Ring" is effective shorthand in political commentary.

Tolkien as the inspiration for the medievalism of others is not limited to derivation, however. The famous agreement between Tolkien and fellow Inkling C.S. Lewis by which the former was to write a tale on time travel, the latter on space travel, resulted in *The Lost Road* and *Out of the Silent Planet*, respectively. However, it is not much of a stretch to assert *The Lord of the Rings*, segments of which were frequently read and criticized in Inkling meetings, and more deeply by Lewis alone, and which Tolkien declared was "a fundamentally religious and Catholic work," inspired Lewis (who was converted to

Catholicism by his friend) to write his own profoundly Christian epic, *The Chronicles of Narnia*. Such has been suggested by Lewis himself. Likewise, Philip Pullman's *Golden Compass*, a very medievalist anti-Christian epic, might easily be construed as a response to the epics of both Inklings. Moreover, Christopher Paolini, author of the acclaimed *Eragon*, is eager to acknowledge his debt not only to Tolkien himself, but to the Germanic and Nordic mythologies to which his readings of Tolkien led him. J.K. Rowling of *Harry Potter* fame referenced Tolkien in her earliest interviews, although later explicitly denied him as an influence. As a figure in the development of modern medievalism, then, Tolkien not only prompts derivative products but provides a model for fantasy texts meritorious in their own right.

Perhaps what is most interesting about Tolkien's medievalism is not his fiction but his own practice of it. Tolkien identified *The Lord of the Rings* as his attempt to create an English national epic, in the sense of Virgil's *Aeneid*, by drawing upon what he believed was the more admirable, heroic nature of not merely the literature but the ideals and aspirations of the medieval English. In the Elves, with their love of nature, penchant for magic, and all but invisible coexistence with the other races of Middle-Earth, we find the Celtic Otherworld. The Rohannese celebrate the Anglo-Saxon warrior mentality in the mead halls and on the battlefield, while the Dwarfs expose the darker side of the Anglo-Saxon vision. Men, especially Aragorn, recall Norman chivalry and courtly love. The Hobbits combine all three: their small stature and hirsute appearance echoing the Dwarfs; their love of nature, simple pleasures, and singing clearly Elvish; their inflated sense of propriety and language reminiscent of the societies of Men. In creating *The Lord of the Rings*, Tolkien moves from being a medievalist to, as the dedicatee of this volume, Professor William Calin, once coined the term, a "medievalismist."

Tolkien was also a medievalist and a medievalismist in his professional life. As the former, his single greatest contribution was undoubtedly his 1936 "The Monsters and the Critics," which single-handedly turned *Beowulf* criticism on its ear and ushered in understanding of the poem as a work of art rather than a relic. This is not to say other criticism and translations (notably his imitative poetic translation of *Sir Gawain and the Green Knight*) haven't been influential: they have. But today, *Beowulf* stands at the center of the medieval canon; before Tolkien, it was read only by specialists at the graduate level. Yet even "The Monsters and the Critics" is not purely scholarly. In his examination of the structure and themes of the epic, Tolkien draws attention to its applicability to the modern sensibility, and the modern dilemma. He finds understanding of the present firmly rooted in the medieval past. This sentiment is further developed in "On Faerie Tales," published in the same volume and quoted in virtually every critical essay on fantasy literature. Here, in defending the significance of faerie (fantasy) tales, Tolkien yearns for the belief in the heroic and magical potential of humanity and the cosmos at large reflected in Celtic myth. To him, faerie is a real and necessary recovery of the goodness reflected in the past as a remedy for the ills of industrialization, cynicism, and inhumanity in the present. It is not a study of ancient Celtic tales but a discovery of what the world of faerie can do for the modern psyche. Tolkien believed in turning to the past to understand and heal the present.

Names in particular signify much in and for Tolkien, from the renaming of Aragorn's sword to denote the "return of the king" and resultant salvation of Middle-Earth, to the appellation of Frodo's home "Bag End," an English translation of the French "cul de sac" (bottom of the bag), which indeed describes its location. Certainly, it is in language that Tolkien makes his most distinctive, if not his best known or most significant, contribution to twentieth-century medievalism. As mentioned above, Tolkien invented languages in his (re)creation of Middle-Earth. Perhaps his best known is Elvish, which has drawn a fanatical following for decades to the point that one can find on the Internet everything from dictionaries and grammars, to a complete translation of the Book of Genesis in this fictional tongue.

Aficionados speak it in club meetings and conferences, much in the way Star Trek fans will converse in Klingon, but with the distinction that it is based on real (Celtic) languages and grammars. Languages—legitimate, fully realized languages—were necessary to Tolkien's creation of a past, frequently recognized only through philology, for Middle-Earth. And without a past, Middle-Earth was mere fiction, not myth.

While Tolkien's contribution to medievalism in both the scholarly and popular realms stands unchallenged and unmatched, it is perhaps fitting to conclude with a note on his personal medievalism. So strongly did he believe in the regenerative power of medievalism that Tolkien, in life, referred to himself as Beren to his beloved wife Edith's Luthien, the archetypal lovers of his mythos, a fact reflected on their joint tombstone. Perhaps he was too modest: for medievalists; for medievalismists; for scholars of fantasy, film, and popular culture; for the fans of his fiction, Tolkien himself is far more iconographic of the Middle Ages than Beren, his love affair with his wife, and with all things medieval, far more courtly than Beren's with Luthien. For Tolkien is not merely the "Author of the Century," he is the father of medievalism.

Bibliography

Chance, Jane. *Tolkien and the Invention of Myth*. Lexington: UP of Kentucky, 2004.

Flieger, Verlyn. *A Question of Time: J.R.R. Tolkien's Road to Faerie*. Kent: Kent State UP, 1997.

Shippey, Tom. *The Road to Middle-Earth: How J.R.R. Tolkien Created a New Mythology*. Boston: Houghton Mifflin, 2003.

---. *J.R.R. Tolkien: Author of the Century*. London: HarperCollins, 2000.

Tolkien, J.R.R. *The Hobbit*. Boston: Houghton Mifflin, 2001.

---. *The Lord of the Rings*. New York: Houghton Mifflin, 1994.

---. *The Monsters and the Critics and Other Essays*. London: Harper Collins, 1983.

Shakespeare: Making Medieval Character

E.L. Risden

Tolkien wrote in a letter in 1954 of "the disastrous debasement of the word [Elves], in which Shakespeare played an unforgivable part" (185), and around 1951 he expressed that sentiment more richly as a curse: "a murrain on Will Shakespeare and his damned [C]obwebs" (143). I once asked Tom Shippey what Tolkien thought of Shakespeare's place in literary history, and he replied wryly that Tolkien thought the Bard "a young writer who shows some promise." We distrust those we fear don't approach with High Seriousness the same materials we do, and Tolkien demanded a carefully and intimately shaped fictional world. Shakespeare's Hamlet comes across as more a Renaissance (or even Romantic) prince than a medieval one, and, while like Samuel Johnson I love Shakespeare, I share Tolkien's dissatisfaction with his means of getting Burnam Wood to march on Dunsinane, and I especially dislike his transformation of Chaucer's Cressid from a fearful widow to a leering tart (though Henryson must share part of that blame). Certainly we owe Shakespeare thanks for powerfully recasting a number of medieval tales for the English Renaissance stage, and while the damage he did to elves took three centuries to repair, his greatest gift to students of medievalism comes not in how he reshaped medieval literature, but in what he did with medieval history (as he knew it). I wouldn't argue for the greatness of the Henry VI plays as plays, but I would suggest that his evolution of Henry V gives us one of our most significant windows on the movement from medieval to modern character, one that defies partisanship and chauvinism and that elbows out creative space for subsequent writers interested in building compelling but believable characters in medieval settings. Our sense of the humanity of the full medieval hero, the glorious accomplishments and stupendous failings, the sense of ambiguity and completeness come as much from Prince Hal as from any other single character in literary history.

The scholar with whom I studied Shakespeare once said that "Shakespeare was true to essential history." I've never quite understood that statement, because I don't know how to separate essential history from inessential history. Perhaps he meant the playwright stayed essentially true to history (i.e., he allowed himself liberties appropriate to dramatic retelling, not egregious, partisan changes of necessary facts). But I suspect he was hinting (and wanted me to infer) that playwrights may adjust recorded details (which we can't trust as "facts" in the modern sense anyway, since they come from a time that precedes any notion of "scientific" history) to create the quality of character and complexity of idea that can blast away audiences' complacencies and urge us to rethink how our peculiar understanding of the medieval past inflects our present. Shakespeare showed us what we needed to see to make sense of why persons had done what they did and how his time had got to where they were in history.

In *Henry IV*, Part 1, Act I, scene 2 concludes with Hal telling us in soliloquy that he is only feigning idleness, that when the time comes he will rise like the sun to everyone's surprise and joy, seeming the better by comparison with his younger days. Should we read the lines in a Postmodern sense of definition by opposition, in a Modern sense as an irony of human nature, in a medieval sense of willful evil and thus notable sin, or in a Renaissance, Greenblattian sense of careful, pragmatic fashioning of a public self? The complexity's the thing wherein we catch the character of the king. At the beginning of Act II, scene 4, when Hal and Poins play a silly joke on the poor "puny drawer" Francis (line 30), do we see a smallness, a meanness of spirit, or do we hear a fore-echoing of events to come? When in the last scene of *Henry IV*, Part 2, Hal dismisses Falstaff with "I know thee not, old man, fall to thy prayers" (V.5.47) do we hear a youth whose heart has hardened to an old companion, or do we hear a king who leaves behind the worst part of himself to accept the status of hero and become the leader his country needs? In *Henry*

V, Act IV, scene 3, in the famous St. Crispin's day speech, does Henry mean literally what he says when he asserts that "he to-day that sheds his blood with me/ Shall be my brother; be he ne'er so vile" (lines 61-62) . . .? Will he generously make all his soldiers nobles, or is he scratching the last bit of battle out of them by raising pointless hopes? In Act V, scene 2, when Henry swears his devotion to Katherine, is he experiencing the medieval, courtly arrow of sudden but true passionate love, or is he further calculating his means to ease himself into the throne of France as well as England? As hero and as king he succeeds: he wins his objectives and unites two countries—but as the Chorus tells us in the Epilogue, his success won't last: he died young and left only an infant son in his place, whose disastrous managers "made his England bleed" (line 12). Henry is neither simply good nor bad, neither a mirror for magistrates nor an exemplary damnable sinner. He has courage, brains, abilities, the "gift of gab"; he grows, he matures, he acts as events require of him. He comes to life not as a medieval type, but very nearly as a man, and a modern one at that. Shakespeare fills the space for character that Chaucer opened up in *The Canterbury Tales*. His dramatic portrait becomes not a presentation of a medieval man, but powerful medievalism that changed our perceptions as well as our literature.

If T.S. Eliot was right in "Tradition and the Individual Talent," each of us remakes literary history every time we read or write or something new: each reading experience changes us and changes our audience, readers and students, and each new composition changes the writer and his or her past and future work. The best authors most thoroughly fulfill and expand our sense of a time, its persons, its nature, its zeitgeist. Their truth to history comes in the realization of their characters on the stages of their time and in our subsequent re-embodiment of their perceptions. As Samuel Johnson wrote, Shakespeare's characters are not simply individuals: each one grows into a species, a person with depth, range, and perpetually intriguing variability. Shakespeare better than anyone else brought the medieval human being back to life, so that in the reading and performance of his work we may do the same. He taught us how to take medieval characters and make them ours.

Bibliography

Shakespeare, William. *The Riverside Shakespeare*. Ed. G. Blakemore Evans, et al. Boston: Houghton Mifflin, 1974.

Tolkien, J.R.R. *The Letters of J.R.R. Tolkien*. Ed. Humphrey Carpenter and Christopher Tolkien. Boston: Houghton Mifflin, 2000.

Christine de Pizan as Maker of the Middle Ages

Barbara K. Altmann

At first glance, the reader might be justified in thinking I misunderstood the premise of this volume. Why would I propose Christine de Pizan (c. 1364-1430) as a "maker" of the Middle Ages? Chronologically and stylistically, she is the successor of Guillaume de Machaut; the contemporary of Jean Froissart, Eustache Deschamps, and, not incidentally, Geoffrey Chaucer; and the precursor of Alain Chartier, the Rhetoriqueurs, and the woman poets of the French and Italian Renaissance.

One could argue that Christine helped "make" the Middle Ages by introducing new elements into the realm of conventional courtly poetry and allegory. While there is much to admire in her work, her biggest innovation was no more and no less than to add a woman's voice—undisguised and generally unapologetic—to the otherwise exclusive and exclusively male voices shaping the cultural production of her day. The persona she cultivated as woman poet and scholar was carefully forged from components familiar to her audience—among them, author portraits mirroring standard images, humility *topoi* in dedications to patrons, fictional interactions with dignified and recognizable allegorical figures—but cloaked in a chaste blue dress and modest, white, head covering. Other medieval authors ventriloquized the lady's voice, while Christine anchored the authenticity of hers on the incontrovertible fact of her biological sex and her experiential knowledge of the world as a woman.

One novel element she introduced into her literary persona was her Italian heritage. At the beginning of the *Book of Deeds of Arms and of Chivalry* (*Livre des fais d'armes et de chevalerie*), she invokes "the wise lady Minerva," goddess of arms and chivalry, as her guarantor that even a simple woman could write with authority about war. She allies herself with the goddess on the basis of their shared origins, as well: "like you," says she, "I am an Italian woman." Her insistence on that common heritage is, of course, an elegant means of sharing in Minerva's wisdom, but it also gestures toward the movement of literary styles and content through Italy to France and beyond in the late Middle Ages, and she explicitly cites Boccaccio by name in the same passage. Knowing that Christine identifies with her native Italy and its authors allows some insight into the complicated intertextual relationship between, for example, Christine's *The Book of the City of Ladies* (*Le Livre de la cité des dames*, 1405) and Boccaccio's *Of Famous Women* (*De mulieribus claris*, 1364).

All very well, one might say, but no matter how much Christine's writerly figure innovates on the conventions of the day, she did no more than many other writers we could list to "make" the Middle Ages. Like Christine, others flattered, beseeched, and tutored the nobility of their day to govern justly. Like Christine, others operated subtle and not-so-subtle transformations on the literary forms they inherited. Like Christine, others helped redefine the dynamic relationship among poet, patron, and manuscript, between composition and performance, between codex as repository and codex as commodity. What, then, sets her apart from so many other "makers"?

The key lies in a small modification of the terms. What if we call Christine not a "maker" of the Middle Ages but the "makings" of the Middle Ages? "Makings" in the sense of what we use to create something, the "stuff" of which something is composed. Christine's work lay mostly fallow for centuries and did not merit the esteem of those nineteenth- and early-twentieth-century makers of literary history who rediscovered the Middle Ages. Approximately fifty years ago, however, a new generation of scholars, led by Charity Cannon Willard, brought Christine back into the conversation. Once scholarly circles knew of her existence, once again began to read her works, she was embraced with a hunger and enthusiasm quite startling in what is sometimes a staid field.

Christine and her large, beautifully produced "oeuvre"

were a tonic. Here was a poet, a woman poet, a daring, successful, prolific, politically-engaged poet, whose work shed light on a whole spectrum of aspects in the life of late-medieval Europe. Her many works lent themselves to examination by literary critics, historians, gender-studies specialists, comparatists, art historians, and codicologists. The texts contained much fodder for study, and the illuminations that accompanied them, well worth serious study in their own right, provided a refined visual face for waxing interest in the "waning" of the Middle Ages.

In short, the reception history of Christine's work in recent decades makes almost as compelling a study as her work itself. I have discussed elsewhere how Christine, along with Joan of Arc and a few select other figures, have become icons of the Middle Ages as we now teach and represent them. Christine's miniatures and some of her texts are a staple of course syllabi, anthologies, calendars, coffee-table books, and send-ups of medieval scholarship.

What is more, she is also the star of a whole range of new cultural artifacts. While she may never enjoy as many versions of the biopic as Robin Hood, King Arthur, or Joan, Christine is well represented in a variety of media. For example, in 2008, BBC radio first broadcast a 75-minute dramatization of Christine's *Book of the City of Ladies* (*Livre de la cité des dames*), the allegorical work with which Christine's name has become largely synonymous. Rebroadcast in September 2010 on BBC 7, this "allegorical fantasy about building a fortress for women from valour, virtue and wisdom" features British actress Kathryn Hunt, known for her role in the long-running soap opera *Coronation Street*. Its listing on the BBC web site is ornamented with a photograph showing in a truncated shot the upper body of a woman, from parted rosy lips to bust, dressed in a coquettish, vaguely Renaissance-style gown. Is this blason intended to portray the generally sedate author, Christine? One of the women who needs refuge in the City? Or perhaps an unexpectedly sensual incarnation of one of the goddesses—Ladies Reason, Rectitude, and Justice—who enlist Christine as their amanuensis?

We might consult the literary portrait of Christine in a recent French historical novel. Matthieu Dhennin's *Saltarello* offers a murder mystery of sorts in which fictional characters rub elbows with the historical. A secondary character, the "delicious woman poet Christine de Pizan" exchanges repartee with Nicolas Flamel, maker and seller of luxury manuscripts, about the misogynistic outrages of the *Romance of the Rose* (*Roman de la rose*) even as her headdress is filched by a mischievous monkey lurking in the rafters of Flamel's workshop. (The description of Christine is from the back cover, my translation; the scene described is on pp. 226-27.) Christine takes center stage in the 2009 Italian film *Christine/Cristina* directed by Stefania Sandrelli, a "true story of a woman who dared to defy power in the name of art" (my translation, back cover of film jewel box). The film premiered at the Fourth International Rome Film Festival in October 2009. Critical reaction has not been favorable, although we might hope that Christine herself would be gratified to have her legacy perpetuated by another cultivated Italian woman in the person of Sandrelli.

These three examples are but a sample. In conclusion, then: like many of her contemporaries, Christine de Pizan worked hard to shape the cultural and political milieu of her day. Her lasting legacy, however, may be that her corpus and her persona, in their many aspects, are proving irresistible, malleable material for the late-twentieth and early-twenty-first centuries as we remake the Middle Ages yet again—inevitably, very much in our own image.

Bibliography

Altmann, Barbara K. "Christine de Pizan, First Lady of the Middle Ages." *Contexts and Continuities: Proceedings of the IVth International Colloquium on Christine de Pizan (Glasgow 21-27 July 2000)*. Ed. Angus J. Kennedy, et al. Glasgow: Glasgow UP, 2002. Pp. 17-30.

Book of the City of Ladies. BBC Radio 7 [http://www.bbc.co.uk/programmes/b007mwc7]. Accessed 31

January 2011.

Blumenfeld-Kosinski, Renate, ed. *The Selected Writings of Christine de Pizan: New Translations, Criticism*. New York: Norton, 1997.

Cerquiglini, Jacqueline. "L'Etrangère." *Revue des langues romanes* 92.2 (1988): 239-51.

Christine de Pizan. *The Book of Deeds of Arms and of Chivalry*. Trans. Sumner Willard, ed. Charity Cannon Willard. University Park, PA: Pennsylvania State UP, 1999.

Dhennin, Matthieu. *Saltarello*. Arles: Actes Sud, 2009.

Willard, Charity Cannon, ed. *The Writings of Christine de Pizan*. New York: Persea, 1994.

---. *Christine de Pizan: Her Life and Works*. New York: Persea, 1984.

B.S. Ingemann (1789-1862): Danish Medievalism of the Early Nineteenth Century

Nils Holger Petersen

Bernhard Severin Ingemann's first historical novel, *Waldemar den Store og hans Mænd* (*Valdemar the Great and his Men*, 1824), a narrative poem written in changing meters, follows the protagonist Duke Valdemar and his struggle to become king of Denmark and to secure the throne for his lineage. The narrative is fairly accurately based on the account in Book XIV of Saxo Grammaticus' chronicle of the Danes, the *Gesta Danorum*, written around 1200. Saxo had been engaged as a chronicler by Archbishop Absalon who, member of one of the most powerful families in Denmark in the twelfth century, was among the faithful supporters of Valdemar during the Danish civil war in the mid-twelfth century. When Valdemar won the day and became king of the entire Danish realm in 1157, Absalon was rewarded with the bishopric of Roskilde (1158-1192). He later became archbishop of Lund from 1177 until his death in 1201. Unsurprisingly, Saxo's account is strongly partial to Valdemar, and so is Ingemann's novel, which adds a particular historiographical ideology (and, of course, many narrative and poetical details). Ingemann made Saxo a figure in his novel (Master Lange, who only toward the end is revealed as Saxo), just as Absalon is called by his assumed original Danish name Axel until almost the end of the novel.

One of the main events during Valdemar's reign (1157-1182) was the canonization of Valdemar's father, Duke Knud Lavard (Canute Lord) who had been murdered by a rival to the Danish throne on 7 January 1131, a week before Valdemar's birth. King Valdemar succeeded in having Knud Lavard canonized by the Pope; St. Knud Lavard was translated into the Benedictine Abbey Church in Ringsted (where King Valdemar was later buried) on 25 June 1170, an occasion when Valdemar also had his young son Knud crowned as the future Knud VI, thus securing the throne for the next generation, though the Danish realm was not hereditary. The celebration in Ringsted has been seen as the manifestation of the Danish Christian monarchy as a fully integrated part of European Latin Christendom.

In Ingemann's novel, St. Knud Lavard is an important reference throughout the narrative. St. Knud is seen as the ideal royal—and saintly—figure. In the very beginning of the poem, Ingemann explicitly evokes figures of the past to tell about their lives and sins in order to admonish "us" and to tell "from where salvation shall come" (*Waldemar den Store*: 3). In crucial situations, St. Knud Lavard even appears as an agent: Ingemann describes, for instance, how St. Knud stands at the side of Valdemar during a battle so that the "son of the saint" carries with him victory and death (153). The story ends, accordingly, with the aforementioned translation of St. Knud and crowning of the young prince Knud, which suggests an intimate connection between the two events: when Absalon tells the king about the papal bull, Valdemar pronounces his saintly father to live again through the seven-year-old prince who, in this way, will be the embodiment of the hopes and ideals which Valdemar has brought to victory in Denmark (361-62). At the actual celebration in St. Bendt's Church in Ringsted, the union of royal and heavenly rule is strongly emphasized, and the moral of the novel is formulated: the "Danish spirit" is awakened by God when pious hearts unite, as they were in the celebration of the two Knud figures (373-74). The novel concludes by pointing out that, while what has been told belongs to the past, Denmark can still become what it has been. Ingemann uses the very same words (arranged slightly differently) as in the very beginning, evoking in particular Bishop Absalon to admonish "us" and point to "salvation" (375). At crucial points in the narrative, Absalon points to Christ, but it is always made clear that Christian salvation for the country has been embodied in the royalty manifested in the figures of St. Knud, Valdemar, and the future King Knud.

King Waldemar and his Men was reviewed in *The Foreign*

Review in 1828, summarizing the contents and translating some lines of the poem. The reviewer is positive but also critical, claiming that Ingemann had tied himself too much to Saxo, thus limiting his poetical freedom. In modern times, very little seems to have been written about Ingemann in English, and few of his works have been translated.

Ingemann, the son of a Lutheran pastor but not a theologian himself, also made an important contribution to Danish hymn writing (as well as serving as a teacher of Danish literature at the *Sorø Academy*, a historical upper school some hundred kilometers outside of Copenhagen). In addition to his series of historical novels—inspired by, but also different from Sir Walter Scott's—continuing Danish history up to the end of the fourteenth century, his hymns belong to the most popular part of his large output in numerous genres. He was a close friend of the—even more famous—nineteenth-century poet/church father/Historian/school man/politician N.F.S. Grundtvig (1783-1872). His hymns have often been criticized for being too vague theologically, perhaps for the same reason they are immensely popular today.

His hymns, especially his morning and evening songs written in the late 1830s, have often been seen as belonging to a completely different, unproblematizing outlook on the world in which God takes care of each individual life, not least children and animals. Ingemann was politically conservative and did not support the democratic process which was introduced with the constitution in 1849. Nicolai Eriksen, however, has argued that Ingemann's use of ideal points in Danish history represents a myth about divine order, manifested in "golden" moments providing the ultimate goal and future of History. In the same way, Ingemann's hymns describe God's providence. Without denying the difficulties of life, providence outweighs any temporary problem. The historical narratives focus on the struggle, but ultimately, according to Eriksen, both reflect a view of overall harmony as a divinely promised ultimate future (and mythic past) already revealed, thus providing Ingemann's "us" with faith and confidence.

Ingemann's medievalism and his theology may then be two sides of the same coin: In one of his most famous evening songs, Heaven is sketched as a medieval castle ("a castle in the west") sheathed with golden shields, where the sun sets every night.

Bibliography

Anon. "Art IV: *Valdemar den Store og hans Mænd,* Valdemar the Great and his Men: An Epic Poem, by B.S. Ingemann. Copenhagen." *The Foreign Review* 2 (1828): 67-79.

Eriksen, Nicolai. "Mellem kosmos og fædreland–et blik på B.S. Ingemanns salmer og historiske romaner." *Transfiguration: Nordisk tidsskrift for kunst og kristendom* 1 (1999): 87-116.

Gjesing, Knud Bjarne. "B.S. Ingemann Biography." *Dictionary of Literary Biography* (2005-2006). [http://www.bookrags.com/biography/b-s-ingemann-dlb]. Accessed 30 January 2011.

Ingemann, B.S. *Waldemar den Store og hans Mænd: Et episk Digt.* Copenhagen: Andreas Seidelin, 1824.

Ingemann, B.S. *Waldemar Surnamed Seir, or the Victorious,* trans. by A Lady. 3 vols. London: Saunders & Otley, 1841.

Nielsen, Marita Akhøj, "B.S. Ingemann: Forfatterportræt." *Arkiv for Dansk Litteratur, http://www.adl.dk/adl_pub/omadl/cv/OmAdl.xsql?nnoc=adl_pub* (retrieved 30 January 2011).

Rossel, Sven H. "Midnight Songs and Churchyard Ballads: the Other Ingemann. A Study in Danish 'Gothic' Romanticism." In: *Vänbok. Festgabe für Otto Gschwantler zum 60. Geburtstag,* ed. Imbi Sooman. Vienna: Verband der Wissenschaftlichen Gesellschaften Österreichs, 1990. Pp. 237-64

Errol le Cain's Fairy Tales as Manuscript Illumination

Veronica Ortenberg West-Harling

Errol Le Cain's (1941-1989) first illustrated book, *King Arthur's Sword,* was published in 1968 and started his career as an illustrator of children's books. Born and educated in Singapore, Le Cain lived in India for five years, travelled through the Far East, then moved to England. Most of his fifty books consisted in illustrating work by others, and retelling various classic fairy- and folktales. The illustrations are deliberately consistent with the origin and style of the story they illustrate. Aladdin is inspired by the nineteenth-century imagination of the Arabic or Persian *One Thousand and One Nights;* others are indebted to Russian folktales. Le Cain's own travels no doubt contributed to his use of Indian decorative traditions and of Chinese art. His "medievalist" books are *King Arthur's Sword, Sir Orfeo, Cinderella, Early Britain: The Celts, Romans and Anglo-Saxons, Thorn Rose, The Twelve Dancing Princesses, Molly Whuppie,* based on a poem by Walter de la Mare, and *The Pied Piper of Hamelin*. In *Orfeo* Le Cain illustrated not the original Greek myth, but the Middle English poem. *King Arthur's Sword* and *Early Britain* are the only two books with specific medieval themes, a retelling of the story of Arthur and Excalibur, and a children's history book. Yet all the books carry a strong medievalist flavour in their choice of decoration and visual cues.

Foremost of these is the repeated representation of the fairyland multi-turreted castle, whether as an illustration in the opening or closing pages in *King Arthur's Sword* and in *Molly Whuppie* (where it serves as a contrast to the Giant's house in the forest), or as the main focus of the story in *Thorn Rose, Cinderella,* and *Dancing Princesses*. This leitmotif is joined by a variety of medieval images, most notably in *Thorn Rose,* where the opening page weaves in pictures based on late medieval French and

Italian costumed ladies standing in front of a tent with pennant, as seen in the Lady with the Unicorn tapestries or in paintings by Uccello, or moving about in a millefleurs landscape of the kind often seen in tapestries of hunting or courtly love parties. The next page fairy procession, travelling through the forest at night on a millefleurs carpet, includes a unicorn-riding fairy. The fifteenth-century setting continues through the castle and courtiers' dress style, and harks back to the Gothic parallels of architecture and nature as nature increasingly encroaches on the palace through the growing wall of thorns, until the prince arrives, a hundred years later, chronologically correctly attired in Renaissance clothing, to wake up the princess.

Full-page illustrations in *Orfeo* also refer specifically to a fifteenth-century court: headdresses, caparisoned horses, knights in Crusader tabards. This medieval fantasy style is used by Le Cain for the upper social echelons of king, princesses and courtiers, often seated at banquets, dressed in the appropriate brocades, furs, and headgear. By contrast, a second type of medieval inspiration, used for the "below stairs" folk, for example the castle's kitchen in *Thorn Rose*, or the giant's house in *Molly Whuppie*, comes from Flemish painting, especially Brueghel, in the peasants' costumes, activities, and human types (the fat cook, the kitchen maid plucking a fowl, the round-faced children). The fullest example of the Brueghel-style is in *Pied Piper*, where the town, centred around a "Grand-Place" seen in the background, includes houses, streets, clothing, and interiors inspired by Flemish paintings, and the Pied Piper himself is a medieval court jester.

But Le Cain rarely took his inspiration from one model. Together with the Flemish, he uses the style of the old German folktale for clothes and interiors in *Molly Whuppie* and *Pied Piper*; a townscape whose walls, houses, and people is reminiscent of the *Book of Hours of Jean de Berry* in *Pied Piper*; and a double-page spread illustration of a battle in *King Arthur's Sword* modelled on the Bayeux Tapestry (as is the Anglo-Saxon lettering in Early Britain). Thus, he remains true to the broad origin of the story in the context of Western Europe, even as he mixes the stylistic inspiration from French, Italian, Flemish, German, and English artistic models. These are direct medieval themes, placed in the body of the text to illustrate the story.

A subtler form of medieval inspiration runs through these books and even through other stories illustrated by Le Cain: his use of illuminated borders around the text, his illuminated initials, and the fonts. In *King Arthur's Sword*, before his Gothic-font title page, the frontispiece contains the customary fairyland castle, seen through a flower border with angels in roundels blowing their trumpets. Illustrations are inset into a decorated initial, with either zoomorphic geometrical patterns or birds inspired from the Insular style. In *Pied Piper*, the opening pages are more clearly modelled on the arches of Anglo-Saxon and Irish Insular manuscripts (*Book of Kells*, *Lindisfarne Gospels*), and illuminated borders frame the text and illustrations, incorporating roundels with pictures of a German or Flemish medieval town. The characteristic illuminated border contains flowers, fruit, animals, or birds, and sometimes anthropomorphized representations of the Sun and Moon, reminiscent of the full page illustrations of manuscripts or millefleurs tapestries, as on the last page of *Pied Piper*. In the forest setting the children led by the Pied Piper are now happily living in the middle of nature, symbolising plenty and truth, in contrast with the hypocrisy and greed of the townspeople.

The most immediate Insular manuscript style is that of *Orfeo*, with a title page almost literally copied from the *Lindisfarne Gospels*, while two other illustrations, both made up of roundels within one main page, mix, in one case, Insular lettering with fifteenth-century manuscript scenes, and in another an imitation of a book such as the *Eadwine Psalter*. Illuminated borders framing the text are a constant feature of Le Cain's work, and they display his medievalist style even in those books whose stories are set in the seventeenth or eighteenth centuries, where dress and furnishings are depicted in that style, as in *Dancing Princesses* and *Cinderella*. The drawings in *Early Britain*, more "realistic," retain the manuscript format, and the frontispiece has a king figure reminiscent of the Christ of the Arrest, and of St John, in the *Book of Kells*. Le Cain said that: "No matter how splendid and exciting the drawings may be, if they work against the story, the picture book is a failure." Using models culled from medieval pictures for stories set in the Middle Ages is entirely appropriate. Yet the medievalist strand extends to his other books, in the decorative style of borders and initials, as well as in the use of the glowing jewel-like colours. Le Cain used his knowledge of medieval artefacts to mix and match styles and themes. His two styles, the ethereal, stylised one, and the more realistic, robust Flemish-painting one, match the two opposing worlds of the stories: the kings and princesses in their castles are drawn in the first, the "real" peasants and burghers in the other, but both remain within the visual vocabulary of the medieval. In addition to his reinterpretation of historically medieval art, Le Cain's models have their ultimate source in manuscript illuminations, a source of inspiration consistent with his taste for rich and vivid colours and vibrant sparkling tones.

Bibliography

Le Cain, Errol. *King Arthur's Sword*. London: Faber & Faber, 1968.
Davies, A. *Sir Orfeo*. London: Faber & Faber, 1970.
Perrault, C. *Cinderella*. London: Faber & Faber, 1972.
Pittenger, W.N. *Early Britain: The Celts, Romans and Anglo-Saxons*. London: Franklin Watts, 1973.
The Brothers Grimm. *Thorn Rose*. London: Faber & Faber, 1975.
---. *The Twelve Dancing Princesses*. London: Faber & Faber, 1975.
De la Mare, Walter. *Molly Whuppie*. London: Faber & Faber, 1983.
Corrin, S. & S. *The Pied Piper of Hamelin*. London: Faber & Faber, 1988.
Biographical information and sample illustrations: www.errollecain.com/

Edna Edith Sayers (f.k.a. Lois Bragg)

Carol L. Robinson

An established medieval scholar, Edna Edith Sayers (formerly, Lois Bragg) is also a woman who has been trapped in the twilight zone between hearing and Deaf cultures, as well as between intellectual brilliance and physical disabilities. Sayer's scholastic contributions to medieval scholarship have often been—like Geoffrey Chaucer's Wife of Bath's Prologue—daring, innovative, humorous, and challenging to both the intellect and the soul. Thus, while she does not directly contribute to medievalism studies, medievalism is one of the best ways to describe the very act of her scholarly (and pedagogical) contributions: what Richard Utz calls "academic medievalism."

Sayer's early scholastic contributions (particularly those that serve as acts of medievalism) included articles with titles like "Sir Gawain and the Green Knight and the Elusion of Clarity" (1985), "Whaleroads and Meadseats: Four Ways of Translating *Beowulf*" (1986), "*Wulf and Eadwacer, The Wife's Lament,* and Women's Love Lyrics of the Middle Ages" (1989), and "Old English Dual Pronouns and their Poetic Uses" (1989). However, they most significantly began with the publication of her first book, *The Lyric Speaker in Old English Poetry* (1991), seemingly the most comprehensive study of Old English lyric poetry to date. The conceptions of these publications occurred prior to her joining the Deaf academic communities housed by The National Institute of Technology for the Deaf and Gallaudet University; furthermore, the fact that these two schools of higher education for the Deaf hired her and that one of them eventually tenured and promoted her, does not at all point to a desire to have a collective hand in the pot of medieval studies. Indeed, according to Sayers, she was hired despite her interests in medieval studies, not at all because of them. Nevertheless, in bringing Sayers and her medieval scholarship into their folds, these two higher education communities of the Deaf represent (whether they like it or not) a collective hand of a people who have been marginalized both within the space-time continuum of the Middle Ages, as well as by those who study the works of the Middle Ages here and now. In other words, while Sayer's contributions do not represent an aspiration to partial ownership of medieval studies by two cultures—the general and more vaguely described disabled populations and the elite academic society found within Deaf/deaf populations—these contributions do represent a partial ownership nonetheless.

I cannot say that Sayers was aware of this intellectual and physical plight, but I suspect that she was.

Why else would the next phases of her scholastic career involve not only major contributions to the development of Deaf culture studies, including a definitive text primer (2001), quality essays involving studies of sign languages (1997), and, ultimately to complete another groundbreaking book that establishes her as a leading scholar of Disabilities in the Middle Ages (2004)? Perhaps the biggest hint to this self-awareness might be found in one of her most recently published book chapters, "Experience, Authority, and the Mediation of Deafness: Chaucer's Wife of Bath" (2010). This work boldly asks "why is her deafness 'scathe' if in fact it neither dampens her sunny self-image nor inhibits her breezy independence or lively social life?" In pointing out an alternative (ironic) reading of Chaucer's use of the word "scathe," Sayers forces the contemporary scholar into a mirror-facing type of self-confrontation of the established pity with which contemporary society often burdens disabled individuals. In other words, she argues that the imposition of contemporary (often disrespectful) perspective of the disabled individual as a noble, yet simultaneously undignified, individual by medieval scholarship upon medieval works is an unworthy type of academic medievalism: shame on us.

Sayers is known by her colleagues for her rhetorical slaps. She rarely couches such even-handed criticism with much padded softness; however, she balances these wys woman observations with slightly self-evasive, anarchical/comical observations. Again, in her writing about the Wife of Bath, she states, "Experience vs authority, rhetoric vs logic, more broadly orality vs literacy, English vs Latin, wives vs husbands—all these battles are suspended when one is deafened." Born hard-of-hearing, eventually becoming stone-deaf, later also endowed with the "gift" of Multiple Sclerosis, surely she has found herself in similar battles, particularly in her work between experience and authority. And yet, for her, neither her deafness nor her M.S., neither in her scholarship nor in her teaching, have suspended such battles.

On the first day I met Dr. Sayers, I had the opportunity to observe and participate in an undergraduate level class devoted to the works of Geoffrey Chaucer. Often, a culture whose language, such as American Sign Language, has no written form—particularly in a world dependent upon (even addicted to) the written word, adopts the dominating culture's already established written form, even though it is in an entirely different language. (For example, the Irish adopted written Latin to relay their medieval Celtic stories, and long before Alfred the Great Anglo-Saxon oral traditions were transcribed into either Latin or Old Norse.) Dr. Sayers seemed to approach teaching Geoffrey Chaucer's works with this knowledge in hand. She and her small band of Deaf English majors, huddled in a circle, referred to the Middle English texts on their desks as they discussed narrative structure, themes, motifs, language, and poetics in American Sign Language. The experience for me was a silent, double-vision (sign language and written text) kind of moment, and I felt as though I had been submerged into an alternate reality, experiencing a living moment of medievalism, while it was in the making!

Sayers concludes in her article on the Wife, "Thus, not only does authority fail to extend its hegemony over the deafened Wife in being quite unable to exhort her, but she fails authority, being now impervious to it. Deafness does not resolve the opposition between experience and authority, but rather forces its abandonment, which seems to be exactly what Chaucer did in the few years remaining to him after he left off his grand experiments with the Wife of Bath." As with Chaucer's portrayal of the fictional Wife of Bath, my portrayal of the living and breathing Edna Edith Sayers is not intended in a romantically foolish light; this isn't the condescending story of a woman's triumph over her disabilities. Unlike Chaucer's narrative, this essay isn't about feminism, nor is it about disabilities studies. This essay is about how these secondary and marginalized bits of reality contribute to a unique form of medievalism, developed by a unique scholar and professor.

Bibliography

Bragg, Lois. "Sir Gawain and the Green Knight and the Elusion of Clarity." *Neuphilologische Mitteilungen* 86 (1985): 482-88.

---. "Whaleroads and Meadseats: Four Ways of Translating Beowulf." *Humanities Education* 3 (1986): 63-77.

---. "*Wulf and Eadwacer, The Wife's Lament,* and Women's Love Lyrics of the Middle Ages." *Germanisch-Romanische Monatsschrift* 39 (1989): 257-68.

---. "Old English Dual Pronouns and their Poetic Uses." *Language and Style* 22 (1989): 337-49.

---. *The Lyric Speaker in Old English Poetry*. Rutherford, NJ: Fairleigh Dickinson UP, 1991.

---. "Visual-Kinetic Communication in Europe before 1600: A Survey of Sign Lexicons and Finger Alphabets prior to the Rise of Deaf Education." *Journal of Deaf Studies and Deaf Education* 2 (1997): 1-25.

---. *Deaf World: A Historical Reader and Primary Sourcebook*. New York: New York UP, 2001.

---. *Oedipus borealis: The Aberrant Body in Medieval Iceland*. Rutherford, NJ: Fairleigh Dickinson UP, 2004.

Sayers, Edna Edith. "Experience, Authority, and the Mediation of Deafness: Chaucer's Wife of Bath." In: *Disability in the Middle Ages*. Ed. Joshua Eyler. Surrey, UK: Ashgate, 2010.

Margaret Atwood and Chaucer: Truth and Lies

Pam Clements

Margaret Atwood is not generally thought of as a writer engaging in medievalism. She has written several novels that some have called science fiction or speculative fiction, but not medievalism. However, one of these, *The Handmaid's Tale,* whose title echoes *The Canterbury Tales,* can be described not only as a work of medievalism, but of neomedievalism. By neomedievalism, I refer to texts that employ medieval references, themes, and materials at several removes from any sort of medieval "originals." In this case, the novel is a near-future dystopia, in which a fundamentalist religious sect has taken over part of the United States and formed a theocracy named Gilead. The body of the novel consists of a first-person narrative by a woman known only as Offred (Of-Fred; she has been assigned as a Handmaid to a Commander, and so takes his name). Atwood's fictional future is a contemporary feminist's nightmare, a pastiche of patriarchies across centuries and cultures. A major theme evokes the fragility of women's rights in the face of ongoing, and intersecting, patriarchies. Yet the "Historical Notes" that follow the main text of the novel introduce another critical theme as Atwood upends the preceding narrative to reveal the complex relationship of story-telling, truth, fiction, and textual transmission.

These "Historical Notes" are supposedly part of the proceedings of a scholarly conference on Gileadean Studies, occurring more than a century after the events of the narrative. Appended to Offred's *Tale,* they lead to a serious warning about the nature of "stories," whether fiction or history, true or false. For, having been drawn into Offred's story of her capture and indoctrination, her growing resistance and attempt to escape, the reader discovers that what she has just read is a *text,* a reconstruction of (fictional) history, an item that one scholar, Professor Pieixoto, even "hesitates to call a 'document'." Atwood thus leaves two medieval clues in her text: a reference to Chaucer within the "Historical Notes" section as well as her title, reminiscent of *The Canterbury Tales*. Such hints lead to a reading of *The Handmaid's Tale* that emphasizes the problem of language as a vehicle for meaning, the very problem Chaucer explores throughout *The Canterbury Tales*: the tension between *ernest* and *game*.

A neomedieval reading points to some striking correspondences between the two works. Making woman's place in society a central feature of her dystopian world, Atwood echoes the *querelle des femmes* that informs so many of Chaucer's *Tales*. Certainly, Gilead's patriarchal social system echoes medieval ideas about women, ideas that make up much of the debate embedded in Chaucer's *Canterbury Tales*. Yet, while the restrictions on women's agency, the veils and lack of access to literacy suggest aspects of the Middle Ages, the novel decenters medieval patriarchy, making it distinctly and disturbingly modern. Gender roles are enforced by cattle prods and computer manipulation of bank accounts.

More importantly, however, the textual history of Offred's story is similar to that of the *Canterbury Tales*. Offred's story has been found recorded on several ancient rock-and-roll cassette tapes that have been ordered in much the same way as the "fragments" of the *Canterbury Tales*. No one can determine Offred's "authorial intent;" her work is an indeterminate text in much the same way as Chaucer's, and her editors fuss over the ordering of the tapes, just as Chaucer scholars have debated the Bradshaw shift. Offred's narrative, then, is anything but a stable text, and her editors seem to enjoy manipulating the pieces.

Like *The Canterbury Tales*, *The Handmaid's Tale* is also as much about storytelling as about its own subject matter. Beyond the question of "sentence" or underlying moral truth in individual tales is the much-discussed problem of "meaning" for the *Canterbury Tales* as a whole. Storytelling as a means of truthtelling, for Chaucer, is eternally fraught. In *The Handmaid's Tale*, Offred similarly doubts her ability to tell the truth about her situation. For one thing, her view is extremely restricted, her information completely controlled by the theocratic elite. Her story must be constructed/deconstructed/reconstructed in her head. Second, she juxtaposes memories of the past with more recent recollections. Third, in a world so completely altered, she can no longer read the past clearly, although she feels it imperative to remember as much and as precisely as she can. Finally, her story is so painful, she resists telling it with a force almost equal to that requiring her to speak.

Offred's knowledge of the new regime is limited to her indoctrination and to what she can glean from her restricted circumstances. Handmaids leave their Commanders' homes only to go marketing; they leave their rooms only for the Saturday night Ceremony. Offred is allowed glimpses of television news, but the media, clearly controlled by the government, is not to be trusted. Consequently, she knows little about the outside world of Gilead. Offred is also trying to fill large memory blanks by telling her story. "There must have been needles, pills, something like that. I couldn't have lost that much time without help" (39). Repeating, "This is a reconstruction. All of it is a reconstruction" (134), Offred keeps reminding the reader that, without "history," without any physical evidence of her pre-Gileadean past, it is only with her receding memory that she can resist her present, or even understand it. In adapting to her new circumstances, Offred has learned, like a good postmodern theorist, that "Context is all" (144).

As much as she wants to tell the truth, Offred also has to resist her own tendency to elaborate, alter, or eliminate events. She recognizes fully the subjectivity of narrative, especially autobiography. In relating her first illicit meeting with her Commander, Offred describes devising ways to kill him, then offers, "In fact I didn't think about anything of the kind. I put it in only afterwards. As I said, this is a reconstruction" (139-40). She also gives two fictional versions of her first sexual encounter with Nick, the Guardian. She punctuates the two versions with corrective comments: "I made that up. It didn't happen that way" (261) and "There wasn't any thunder though, I added that in" (263). She finally admits, "It didn't happen that way either . . . . All I can hope for is a reconstruction" (263). As Steven McCabe notes, "Offred is a narrator uniquely suited to juxtaposing truth and lie, euphemism and bluntness, the past and present. Hers is a historian's struggle, an effort to understand the present by comparing it to the past" (31). Like Chaucer, Atwood plays with the many ways truth can be embedded in fiction, and with the ways fictions or histories can disguise or warp the truth.

Atwood's self-consciousness is even more apparent in the "Historical Notes." The scholars, treating Offred's story purely as a *text*, ignore the "truth" of her tale. Editors Wade and Pieixoto are more interested in arranging their manuscript fragments and determining the probable identity of Offred's Commander than they are in hearing Offred's story. With apparent scholarly detachment, Pieixoto says, "we must be cautious about passing moral judgment upon the Gildeadeans" (302). Janet Karsten Larson notes that "The passionate immediacy of the Handmaid's witness is muffled in a talk spiced with 'harmless' sexist jests that should give the game away" (498).

Like *The Canterbury Tales, The Handmaid's Tale* shows that distinguishing between *ernest* and *game, sentence* and *solaas* is not always an easy task. For Atwood, as for Chaucer, texts must contain meanings, although imparting and reading those meanings is, ultimately, always uncertain.

Bibliography

Atwood, Margaret. *The Handmaid's Tale*. Boston: Houghton Mifflin, 1986.

Chaucer, Geoffrey. *The Canterbury Tales*. Ed. F.N. Robinson. 2nd ed. Boston: Houghton Mifflin, 1957.

Grace, Dominick M. "*The Handmaid's Tale*: 'Historical Notes' and Documentary Subversion." *Science-Fiction Studies* 25.3 (1998): 481-94.

Howard, Donald. *The Idea of the Canterbury Tales*. Berkeley: U of California P, 1976.

Larsen, Janet Karsten. "Margaret Atwood's Testaments: Resisting the Gilead Within." Rev. *The Handmaid's Tale*. In: *The Christian Century* (May 20-27, 1987): 496-98.

McCabe, Stephen. "A Novel for the Complacent." Rev., *The Handmaid's Tale*. In: *The Humanist* (September/October 1986): 31-32.

Bernhard Ten Brink and German English Studies in Lotharingia

Richard Utz

Did you know that "birtherist" thinking is not limited to adherents of the Tea Party? One of the results of the rampant nationalism that infiltrated the academy in the second half of the nineteenth century is that we have developed an obsessive need to attribute national origin to our scholarly forbears based on their place of birth. In fact, the more successful and famous the scholar, the more competition there will be about claiming him *pro domo* after his passing. Consider the case of Bernhard/Barend Egidius Konrad ten Brink who, born in Amsterdam on January 12, 1841, and son of a Dutch father and a German mother, has been called an eminent Dutch Anglicist by English, Swiss, and Dutch sources and a German through and through by his German colleagues. In this, as in numerous other cases, birth places, birth certificates, parents' nationalities, passports, or nationalist etymologies of first and last names need to be contextualized with the scholar's own actual pronouncements and practices. As soon as we do that, Bernhard ten Brink reveals himself as a staunchly German figure whose academic work well mirrors the nationalistic fervor of his time.

His appointment as the first chair of English Philology at the *Reichsuniversität* Straßburg, an institution expressly constructed by the imperial government in Berlin to re-Germanize Alsace-Lorraine after the Franco-Prussian war of 1871, placed him at the center of a fascinating cultural conflict. At first sight, his multilingual background (Dutch, French, German, English) should have made him a conciliatory figure in bilingual and bicultural Straßburg/Strasbourg. Moreover, his decision to keep on lecturing on French subject matter in the absence of sufficient demand for classes in the new subject of English should also have positioned him well with those who saw the new university on the soil of medieval Lotharingia as a place uniquely predestined to unite, not divide, French and German culture. However, while ten Brink insisted on making incursions into the field of the Straßburg chair of Romance philology, Eduard Böhmer, he sought out his academic allies among some of the most openly Germanizing colleagues, especially Wilhelm Scherer, a Germanist with whom he coedited the book series, *Quellen und Forschungen zur Sprache und Culturgeschichte der germanischen Völker*. His appointment as *Rektor* (President) of the university in 1890 would indicate that he made a smart political choice by joining the more influential faction of the Straßburg professoriat.

Of course, a critical view of ten Brink's nationalist predilections should not keep us from recognizing his substantial achievements as a medievalist. A student of the famed Romance philologists, Friedrich Diez and Nicolaus Delius, his appointment as chair of the first professorship in English philology in all of Europe became the starting signal for English as a university subject to extricate itself from its position as a lesser sister to Germanic, Romance, and Classical studies. Ten Brink's scholarship, just like Julius Zupitza's at the Humboldt University in Berlin, was representative of the first generation of modern academic English studies world-wide. Conscious of the scholarly reputation conveyed by publications about canonical texts and writers, ten Brink concentrated his efforts on *Beowulf,* Chaucer, and Shakespeare, and rather than spending his time on numerous essays and shorter studies, he focused on the monograph and literary history as his preferred media of scholarly communication. Whereas Zupitza made his reputation with the help of Lachmannian manuscript study and a widely-used anthology of Old and Middle English texts for the classroom, ten Brink produced a triad of monographs, *Chaucer: Studien zur Geschichte seiner Entwickelung und zur Chronologie seiner Schriften* (1870), *Beowulf: Untersuchungen* (1888), and *Chaucers Sprache und Verskunst* (1884), all three of which became canonized classics for students of early English literature.

If positivism, (old) historicism, and philology are nowadays in disrepute as dated, drab, and dry-as-dust enterprises, ten Brink's scholarship discloses the excitement nineteenth-century philological paradigms could engender among their first practitioners in the young discipline of English studies. While we may want to smile, from a distance of more than a century, about his earnest attempt at finding the virtues of Classical verse in Chaucer, his 1870 *Chaucer Studien* is without doubt the first systematic study of Chaucer's prosody. As such, it greatly stimulated the study of the father of English poetry in Europe and North America, especially among the members of Frederick Furnivall's Chaucer Society. Far from erecting a *cordon sanitaire* between the late medieval writer and his own age, one can sense in ten Brink's investigations the deep desire to turn his beloved subject of investigation into a premodern philologist, a man who, had he only felt less akin to Dante and Boccaccio and more akin to the (early) modern and philological Petrarch, could have achieved even more than he did.

Unlike many of his scholarly contemporaries, ten Brink keenly recognized that there was an audience outside the universities that was ready to learn about Britain and English literature. In his philological history of English literature (*Geschichte der englischen Literatur*, 1877), also a first in the academic study of English, ten Brink gave himself leave to connect the rhetorical and linguistic basis of his philological work with some of the aesthetic, biographical, historical, political, and social mainstays of literary history. The result is an enthusiastic melange of the very nationalism and philology already palpable in the pious dedication of his critical edition of Chaucer's "General Prologue" to the *Canterbury Tales* to the Emperor Wilhelm I in 1871. In his *Geschichte*, the aspects of early English texts most celebrated are the ones that seem to lead away from foreign (French) influence and toward a somehow evolutionarily advanced postmedieval Germanity. Had Chaucer had occasion to write a story for the Yeoman, ten Brink opines, dim recollections of the Germanic past, including the storm god Wodan, would have welled up in such a Canterbury narrative.

We find then, in ten Brink's work, as high a degree of desire for making medieval writers and texts his own as we see in the perhaps more sophisticated approaches of late twentieth- and twenty-first-century critics. If the late-nineteenth-century positivist philologist participated willingly in the dominant nationalist discourse of his day, today's scholars have found a rich terrain for sublimation within various contemporary historicisms, feminisms and, above all, psychoanalysis. This is why I am convinced that an essay on La(ca)ncelot would not shock ten Brink, but I know he would be scandalized to find that it appeared in a North American journal and not in *Anglia*, *Archiv*, or *Englische Studien*.

Bibliography

Haas, Renate, and Albert Hamm. *The University of Strasbourg and the Foundation of Continental English Studies: A Contribution to a European History of English Studies*. Frankfurt: Lang, 2009.

Kluge, Friedrich. "Bernhard ten Brink." *Jahrbuch der Shakespeare Gesellschaft* 26 (1892): 306-10.

Kölbing, Eugen. "Chronologisches Verzeichnis der von Bernhard Ten Brink Publicirten Schriften, Abhandlungen und Recensionen." *Englische Studien* 17 (1892): 186-88.

Schröer, Arnold. "Aus der Frühzeit der englischen Philologie. I. Persönliche Erinnerungen und Eindrücke." *Germanisch Romanische Monatsschrift* 15 (1925): 32-51.

Utz, Richard. *Chaucer and the Discourse of German Philology. A History of Reception and an Annotated Bibliography of Studies, 1793-1948*. Turnhout: Brepols, 2002; "The Founding Fathers: Julius Zupitza and Bernhard ten Brink" (pp. 73–126).

Fact and Fiction: Marcel Schwob's Archeologies and Medievalism

Gayle Zachmann

In homage to his vast erudition, unswerving humanism, and incisive interrogation of the place and function of literary and symbolic production, Marcel Schwob's medievalism bears witness to a life of committed inquiry. Begun before the age of eleven—the year of his first publication in the republican newspaper, *Le Phare de la Loire*—Schwob's highly crafted and diverse *oeuvre* still defies easy classification. His contributions as scholar, essayist, critic, and *conteur,* however, prove him at the very least a lucid writer of the rise of the Middle Ages and its potential verbal and social consequences.

Over the course of the nineteenth century, medieval studies became a scholarly obsession and a subject of ideological and aesthetic debate. Written testimony to this vogue, Schwob's work at once deploys, documents, and scrutinizes the dissemination of medieval themes and forms. It simultaneously and self-consciously exposes the historical and human sciences that would aspire to interpret them. By the time Schwob was addressing medievalism in the 1890s, archeology—earlier, a feature of romantic travel narratives—was an integral part of nineteenth-century conceptions of historical study and had become, along with the press, a mechanism for popularizing (and sometimes questioning) historical memory and the advances of the sciences. As the Third Republic grappled with its medieval, monarchical, and religious pasts, pavilions with replicas of Frankish ancestors drew crowds and the press at World's Fairs. Indeed, in the press, as in scholarly production and literary texts of the time, heritage, history, and science were often linked to archeologically grounded evidence and legitimizations of memory, the social body, and national identity.

Although his research on Villon presents no example of

social cohesion, Marcel Schwob's studies of the notorious writer's work remain the most prominent aspect of his medievalism. Like the renowned philologist and literary historian Gaston Paris, Schwob practiced a genre of literary archeology that bolstered the historical value of documents and their utility as artifacts or social evidence. Exhibiting the wealth of knowledge to be uncovered in this controversially "vulgar" monument and its language, Schwob's in-depth, archivally-grounded analysis of Villon's *argot* contributed substantially to studies of proto-sociolinguistics and a countercultural group known as the *Coquillards*.

In criticism, too, and particularly in the 1893 *Spicilèges*, an anthology of previously published essays compiled as a poetic testament, Schwob documented the appeal of the Middle Ages as subject matter and endorsed literary explorations of medievalism. Opening in the same way as some of the "lives" in his own *Vies imaginaires*, his essay on Flaubert's *Saint Julien l'hospitalier* announces that little is known of the life of Saint Julian. This lacuna serves as a pretext for the aesthetic and social critic to embark on a historical dig. A figurative excavation of our knowledge to date, the essay provides a philological chronicle of representations of Saint Julian in historical, religious, and literary texts.

Fluent in medieval social structures and the conventions of medieval narrative and terminology, Schwob goes on to detail how Flaubert's tale takes its lead—and simultaneously distinguishes itself—from medieval hagiography. He also notes points of confluence with chivalric romance, citing the hero and his trials, the marvelous presence of animal oracles, penitence, and leper-impersonating angels offering redemption. Schwob emphasizes Flaubert's situation of the narrative in the Middle Ages and the writer's avowed inspiration from the Rouen cathedral's stained glass, noting that earlier written versions of the Saint Julian narrative include terms such as *chevalier, château fort,* and *chatelaine.* In spite of this, his investigation proposes that Flaubert's intervention in the legend of Saint Julian privileges popular folkloric sources that predate the saint's medieval inscription.

Schwob's relationship to the Middle Ages, however, is not limited to scholarly research or archeological criticism. His own family narrative, which traced his maternal line as descendants of Cayms and companions to Louis IX, exemplifies a mode of genealogical historiography characteristic of both nineteenth-century narratives and chivalric texts. This said, Schwob's medievalism does not merely entail testimony to a vogue, recuperating texts for their historical value, nor is his practice one of the disinterested scholar or modern scribe.

Situated in the Middle Ages, Schwob's disturbing 1896 *Croisade des enfants*, a fictionalized chronicle of the tragic 1212 Childrens' Crusade, re-presents the ill-fated journey through touching testimonials by real and imagined witnesses. Multiple intertexts provide documentary evidence for the anecdote, as the chronicle form—along with the mimesis that it conventionally assumes—mingles provocatively with fictive, firsthand testimony. The text's uncanny verisimilitude underscores the instability and the potential of fictive testimony as documentation for a faithful archeology of the event and, by extension, for any crusade. Ending his story with Pope Gregory's call for a memorial monument, Schwob simultaneously puts forth his own document, too, as a verbal stele to the disasters of innocence and ignorance.

In an only somewhat more secular crusade, his 1904 *Moeurs des diurnales,* a satirical treatise on journalism, Schwob questions what and how we can know. Problematizing the role of the modern journalist and the writer in the production of knowledge, Schwob parodies the archeological thinking that characterized and privileged historical inquiry of his era. The pedagogical text, where "chacun de ces courts chapitres a éte rédigé pour vous y aider," clearly maintains a hyperbolic discursive mission as the burlesque nineteenth-century journalistic revival of the antique orator and the enthusiastic medieval preacher mockingly meet in a narrative voice that announces responsibility: "N'oubliez pas que vous êtes devenus les instructeurs du peuple."

In *L'histoire du journal: L'Ile des diurnales*, a key essay of the *Moeurs*, an investigative reporter opens his story with pseudo-news of a fictional, archeological find: a bas-relief and inscription that journalists, philologists, and archeologists were struggling to explain. One journalist (from the Popolo, he notes) proposes that a rather fantastic found text fragment might shed light on the truth of the find. The embedded travel narrative chronicles the observations of an alien eyewitness to life on a mysterious island off Brittany. There, inhabitants worship very singular birds, whose droppings—ink stained parchments—are seen as oracles and venerated as time-sensitive truth. Presented by the journalist as plausible and documentary evidence to decipher the bas-relief and its inscription, the text fragment, a pseudo-artifactual, parodic history of the newspaper, destabilizes the historical value of *la chose vue*, as well as firsthand testimony, archeological interpretations, and *la chose lue*.

Taking journalism, as well as archeological and historical inquiry to task, the *Moeurs* parodies the pretensions to truth of the treatise, along with the knowledge it would disseminate as education. While for many, education reform, medievalism, and archeology combined in a recuperation of history that would support religious education and religious sciences, medieval studies would furnish fodder for all sides of the education debates during the Third Republic. Clearly aligned with such scholars as Gaston Paris and Michel Bréal, Marcel Schwob's work bears witness to the rise of the new discipline. His scholarship and his destabilizing, modern literary production effectively mobilized medieval legends and forms to query archeologies of knowledge, and the signifying power and historical value of erudite fiction.

Bibliography

Allain, Patrice. "Famille Schwob. Des lettres à la République à la République des lettres." *Europe*. No. 925. Mai 2006. 32-49.

Effros, Bonnie. "Selling Archeology and Anthropology: Early Medieval Artifacts at the Expositions Universelles and the Wiener Weltausstellung, 1867-1900." *Early Medieval Europe* 16.1 (2008): 23-48.

Marcel Schwob. *L'Homme au masque d'or.* Paris: Gallimard, 2006.

Perrin-Saminadavar, Eric, ed. *Rêver l'archéologie au XIXe siècle: de la science à l'imaginaire.* Saint-Etienne: Publications de l'Université de Saint-Etienne, 2001.

Ridoux, Charles. *Evolution des études médiévales en France de 1860 à 1914.* Paris: Champion, 2001.

Schwob, Marcel. *Oeuvres.* Ed. Alexandre Gefen. Paris: Les Belles Lettres, 2002.

Albert Robida, Medieval Publicist

Elizabeth Emery

Albert Robida (1848-1926) lavishly employed exclamation points in the descriptions of medieval subjects that appeared in the numerous travel guides, exposition catalogs, and popular histories he wrote and illustrated over the course of his career (some 60,000 drawings and 200 books authored or illustrated). "Dinan!" he marvels, recounting his travels through Brittany by train, coach, cart, omnibus, and boat (*La Bretagne*, 1891): "Tout est superbe!" "Oh vieilles villes je vous aime!" he exclaims in *Les Vieilles Villes d'Italie* (1878). Such interjections breathe life into the cities he describes, restoring decrepit nineteenth-century monuments to an imagined initial splendor. From Italy, Provence, and Spain to Brittany, Normandy, Paris, Flanders, the Rhine, and Switzerland, Robida's books about the old cities of Europe continue to spark the imagination of the armchair tourists who accompany him, who explore the continent's premier heritage sites through his narrative, a personal commentary enriched by sketches featuring those architectural details he considered most interesting or curious. Robida's exclamation points serve as a visual translation of his tireless enthusiasm for these monuments. Indeed, he was one of the most effective publicists medieval France has known.

Good publicists, however, hide behind the success of their campaigns. Such was the case of Robida, remembered less for his work as a medieval enthusiast than as an irreverent caricaturist of contemporary society, as a science fiction author (*Le Vingtième siècle, La Vie électrique, La Guerre au Vingtième siècle*), and as a popular book illustrator. This was as much a result of his broad interests as it was of the audiences he targeted: instead of crowning himself a "father" of medieval studies by writing scholarly tomes intended for erudite reception, his publications were resolutely mass-market: travel books, sketches published in the periodical press, magazines, post cards, and other ephemera calculated to engage the public's imagination, thus encouraging contemporaries to appreciate and preserve the vestiges of the Middle Ages still present in the late nineteenth century.

His travel books may have been inspired by those of Charles Nodier and Isidore Taylor, whose *Voyages pittoresques et romantiques dans l'ancienne France* (1820-1878) served a similar conservational function (they assembled texts, drawings, and watercolors by a number of writers and artists for a public of bibliophiles), but Robida took a different tack. He wrote for the masses, producing more than 200 drawings and 40 lithographs per book by himself and publishing them in affordable editions (*La Bretagne* retailed for two francs). Where Nodier and Taylor's large format illustrations could be removed from the albums and sold individually, Robida's books privileged small vignettes, interspersed within the text itself. Like medieval manuscripts, in which text and image gloss one another, the interplay between text and image in his pages makes subjects tangible. His excitement at encountering a particular architectural detail, like a flamboyant door at Dinan, or a particularly picturesque Gothic church in Rennes, is reinforced by the reader's experience of viewing that detail within the text itself.

If we have forgotten Robida as a "maker" of the Middle Ages today, it is, in part, because of this mass market focus. He was a caricaturist and journalist, a self-taught historian who left school at the age of twelve. Such credentials labeled him a rank amateur by the standards of the scholarly community that published, catalogued, and perpetuated the work of their friends and colleagues during the 1890s.

Yet he has also been forgotten because his single greatest contribution on behalf of the Middle Ages was also one of the most ephemeral. He was the driving force behind the tremendously-successful *Vieux Paris* exhibit of the 1900 Paris World's Fair, a miniature city containing reproductions of famous Parisian buildings "mutilated" or destroyed from the Middle Ages to the eighteenth century: the staircase of the Sainte-Chapelle, the Pont au Change, la Porte Saint-Michel, and La Tour

MORLAIX 159

possède aussi en bas une belle cheminée de pierre à large manteau orné d'un cordon de sculptures.

Ce beau spécimen des riches maisons du Morlaix d'autrefois a bien failli disparaître : on avait décrété sa démolition parce qu'elle commet le crime d'avancer de quelque cinquante centimètres sur l'alignement imposé, il a fallu pour la sauver la croix et la bannière et le cri d'indignation des archéologues.

La *Grande-Rue* heureusement n'a pas été touchée encore, elle est restée telle

Page layout from Albert Robida. *Les Vieilles Villes. Bretagne.* Paris: A la librairie illustrée, 1891. 159. Private

Vieille porte à Dinan. Albert Robida. *Les Vieilles Villes. Bretagne.* Paris: A la librairie illustrée, 1891. 80. Private Collection.

Rennes. Ancienne Eglise Saint Yves. Albert Robida. *Les Vieilles Villes. Bretagne.* Paris: A la librairie illustrée, 1891. 89. Private

du Louvre, to name just a few. Within the walls of *Le Vieux Paris* visitors found a functioning medieval village, replete with taverns, restaurants, a chapel, shops, and wandering minstrels. While recognized medievalists like Viollet-le-Duc (to whose drafting skills Robida's were compared) were hired by the French government to renovate existing components of the national patrimony, Robida constructed—for entertainment purposes—entire urban contexts that had been previously destroyed, only to have them razed once again at the end of the fair.

Throwing himself into his dream project with customary enthusiasm, Robida claimed to have spent a year reading documents in archives and choosing the buildings that would be reconstructed within *Le Vieux Paris*. A team from Les Monuments historiques helped build them (from stone and wood, not cardboard). For Robida, it was not enough to reconstruct the monuments. Just as his enthusiasm for the monuments of Brittany or Provence came from imagining structures from the past surrounded by bustling communities, his *Vieux Paris* teemed with life. Mérovak, the notorious bell-ringer of Notre-Dame de Paris offered carillon demonstrations in the recreated chapel, Saint-Julien-des-Ménétriers, while the Schola Cantorum mounted a variety of early music concerts. Well-known Parisian *chansonniers* performed in the taverns, while costumed shopkeepers sold their wares in the street. Roving actors greeted visitors in Old French. This was not just a professional endeavor on Robida's part, but a passionate personal commitment to bringing the past back to life for his contemporaries. Indeed, Robida's children recollect the intensity with which all members of the family supported the project: embroidering banners, working on sculptures, sewing costumes, and designing menus, accessories, and souvenirs, like postcards, stamps, fans, and elaborate souvenir programs and guide books.

The fair itself was visited by some 51 million visitors, and while it is unlikely that every visitor passed through *Le Vieux Paris*, it was one of the most commercially-successful attractions, suggesting that Robida's temporary creation reached an international population far greater than any scholarly author could ever hope to do. Although the use of exclamation points may not seem a lofty marker for a "maker" of the Middle Ages, Robida's innovative use of new media—comics, travel books, posters, advertisements, stamps, souvenirs, and a theme park attraction—made the treasures of the Middle Ages come alive for a public unfamiliar with more scholarly research. Like a town crier—Oyez, oyez, oyez!—his enthusiasm rang through illustrations, books, and the streets of *Le Vieux Paris,* attracting visitors and inviting them to engage with a medieval period it had considered forever lost. Robida's publications, illustrations, events, and souvenirs internationally publicized the Middle Ages as a pivotal moment in the development of world heritage.

Bibliography

Brun, Philippe. *Albert Robida (1848-1926): sa vie, son oeuvre.* Paris: Editions Promodis, 1984.

Emery, Elizabeth. "Protecting the Past. Albert Robida and the Vieux Paris Exhibit at the 1900 World's Fair." *Journal of European History* 35 (2005): 65-85.

Robida, Albert. *Le Vieux Paris. Guide historique, pittoresque & anecdotique.* Paris: 1900.

---. *Les Vieilles Villes. La Bretagne.* Paris: A la librairie illustrée, 1891.

---. *Les Vieilles Villes d'Italie.* Paris: Dreyfous, 1878.

Le Téléphonoscope. Bulletin des Amis d'Albert Robida. 1998-present.

Le Vieux Paris. Le Parvis St. Julien. Photograph featured on a 1900 World's Fair souvenir postcard. Private Collection.

C.S. Lewis: *More Maiorum*

F. Regina Psaki

Clive Staples Lewis (Belfast 1898-Oxford 1963) was a fellow and tutor of English at Magdalen College in Oxford from 1925 to 1954. In 1956 he went to Magdalene College at Cambridge as the first Professor in Medieval and Renaissance English Literature, a chair created for him. In merely quantitative terms Lewis' influence as an academic medievalist is dwarfed by his impact in popular culture, first as a Christian apologist and then as a writer of fantasy. In comparative Medieval Studies Lewis is best remembered for his large-scale portrayals of medieval intellectual models, portrayals still productive and influential if nuanced by later scholarship.

Lewis was an all-sided intellectual in the best sense of the term, and even a brief look at his activity requires a series of lists. He wrote in multiple categories: medieval literary history; Christian apologetics and polemics; autobiography, letters, and journals; science fiction and allegorical fantasy. He wrote for multiple audiences: academic medievalists; academics from other disciplines; reflective readers engaged with questions of religion; and of course readers of fiction, both adult and juvenile. He took up in writing the most serious ethical, epistemological, and aesthetic issues that humankind has formulated, and kept them urgent and complex, yet clear. The nature of evil and the devil; the medieval world-view; the courtly literary imagination; the place of religion in an increasingly secular world; the salvation narrative in imaginative fiction; the nature of heroism: these could be dire, dense topics. Yet readers do not find *The Screwtape Letters* dry, *The Discarded Image* or *The Allegory of Love* pedantic, or *The Lion, the Witch, and the Wardrobe* simplistic. For each genre and each audience Lewis developed a compelling voice.

In the learned register of humanities scholarship in this new century, Lewis' scholarly voice stands out because he wants to communicate. He wears his powerful erudition lightly; he is solicitous and respectful toward his readers; he frames subtle and abstruse issues in accessible language; he makes good use of a generous and welcome sense of humor. He compares a modern reader who visits the Middle Ages looking only for the familiar, to an Englishman who visits the Continent and "complains of the bad tea where he might have had excellent coffee" (1966, 2). Lewis' prose crackles with energy and glitters with images both precise and alive. He describes the *Divine Comedy*'s relation to (what he saw as) the consuming medieval pursuit of coherence,

> ...the tranquil, indefatigable, exultant energy of a passionately logical mind ordering a huge mass of heterogeneous details into unity. [...] Hence the *Comedy* which is, I suppose, the supreme achievement: crowded and varied as a railway station on a bank holiday, but patterned and schematized as a battalion on a ceremonial parade. (1966, 44)

It is a leaden understatement to note that humanists nowadays do not tend to write scholarship in language this transparent.

Lewis' communicative charge is more than an end in itself, independent of its content; it is the audible voice of the intellectual position it articulates. He wants to communicate with readers about the Middle Ages because the Middle Ages is not merely relevant to us, it is urgent: it *is* us. Lewis reaches an exquisite balance between emphasizing the alterity of the medieval world and emphasizing the continuity between that world and our own. *The Allegory of Love* and *The Discarded Image* limn in deft strokes the specificities of the medieval worldview, the literary vehicles and strategies by which medieval authors expounded it, the network that informs the literary and cultural manifestations of the medieval "model," all in terms that are both unifying—interdisciplinary—and highly specific. Lewis reminds us that medieval terms and concepts can sometimes look deceptively like our own, and that this is precisely when we need to look much closer. But the reason it is necessary and valuable to look much closer is that we still have so much to learn from the period. We can't discard the Middle Ages and its obsessions because we can't say we've resolved any of them. We have to talk about the Middle Ages, and talk and talk some more, so we can't do it in turgid, opaque language that to the specialist is merely dreary and joyless, but to the non-specialist is quite lethal.

If Lewis were alive in 2011 he might ask: When did humanists decide that our material was so very arcane that it could only be expressed in heavily coded terms of art? When did we cut ourselves loose from interested generalist readers, and from colleagues in other disciplines? When did we trade communication for an imagined credibility that depends on obscurity? The "crisis in the humanities"—epistemological and institutional—probably would not have occurred on Lewis' watch. He would have made sure the general public and the political leadership alike knew *exactly* why the humanities matter, why the Middle Ages matter.

Granted, and very importantly, Lewis like most of his intellectual cohort was not especially sensitive to a host of questions which absorb and exercise us today; we need not be nostalgic for a Medieval Studies unresponsive to issues of sex and gender, for example. But then again the innovations he brought to the discipline were necessary, then and now. Courtly love literature is an area that Lewis made visible as a necessary object of study. He articulated the pitfalls of periodization, particularly with regard to the Renaissance (a term now, tellingly, traded in for "Early Modern"). He painted in beautiful words the beauty of the medieval "model" of the physical and metaphysical world, a world run by the impulse of desire rather than that of law and obedience. It is for each generation to bring to intellectual history its own innovations, while trying to retain what was urgent, beautiful, and exalted in the discipline before; Lewis did this successfully in both his scholarship and his fiction.

Lewis was a charismatic, articulate spokesman for approaching the past with a blend of intimacy and critical distance, and for understanding (or at least approaching) our shared preoccupations "in the way of our ancestors," *more maiorum*. His fantasy and science fiction works too illustrate this imperative. Like a medieval poet he uses imaginative fiction to show, scrutinize, and transmit the core values of his worldview to a larger, non-specialist audience. That some of these values reflect the medieval landscape he studied, and others the modern glass through which he saw that landscape, epitomizes the dual focus of every intellectual historian.

Bibliography

Cantor, Norman. "The Oxford Fantasists: Clive Staples Lewis, John Ronald Reuel Tolkien, and Frederick Maurice Powicke." In: *Inventing the Middle Ages: The Lives, Works, and Ideas of the Great Medievalists of the Twentieth Century*. New York: William Morrow, 1991. Pp. 205-44.

Edwards, Bruce L., ed. *C.S. Lewis: Life, Works, and Legacy*. Westport, CT: Praeger, 2007. Vol. 1: *An Examined Life*; Vol. 2: *Fantasist, Mythmaker, and Poet*; Vol. 3: *Apologist, Philosopher, and Theologian*; Vol. 4: *Scholar, Teacher, and Public Intellectual*.

Lewis, C.S. *Studies in Medieval and Renaissance Literature*. Cambridge: Cambridge UP, 1966.

McSwain, Robert and Michael Ward, eds. *The Cambridge Companion to C.S. Lewis*. Cambridge: Cambridge UP, 2010.

Ward, Michael. *Planet Narnia: The Seven Heavens in the Imagination of C.S. Lewis*. Oxford: Oxford UP, 2008.

The Medievalism of Charles Eliot Norton

Kathleen Verduin

The two solid, dignified volumes, bound in sober taupe and titled *The Letters of Charles Eliot Norton*, stood like a double fortress in one of the ninety-odd orange crates that housed the library of Leslie J. Workman: a library more of old books than new, collected from countless visits to the Salvation Army and the Goodwill where, as I would discover in the years of our marriage, Leslie would forage for hours and then emerge triumphant with box upon box of fifty-cent finds. "A Dante scholar," I murmured, hoping to sound intelligent. "Yes," he replied. "A man kind of like me. Had trouble fixing on a career, found himself rather late. Always wanted to write a book about him."

Leslie's interest in Norton stretched far back, to a time long before I knew him, perhaps even before he met Bill Calin at the Kalamazoo Congress in the 1970s: and although I doubt that Leslie really had much in common with Norton, I suspect that Norton functioned for him as a kind of totemic ancestor, presiding benevolently over *Studies in Medievalism*, the journal that Leslie founded against all odds and to which Bill Calin has contributed so much. For as Bill will attest, Leslie was in some ways a nineteenth-century man: certainly he loved the great Victorian scholars with their book-lined studies and magisterial forays into history. And besides, Norton (1827-1908), a gentleman scholar until his appointment as Professor of Fine Arts at Harvard at the age of forty-six, had ultimately risen to prominence as the preeminent medievalist of his day, contributing prodigiously to the establishment of medieval studies as an academic discipline and promoting attention to what he called "that grand period, the Middle Ages" through all the avenues open to him.

Son of the "Unitarian Pope" and philologically inclined Andrews Norton (1786-1853) and nephew of George Ticknor (1791-1871), the first to teach Dante at Harvard, Norton was immersed from childhood in the medievalism of his century—a "great intellectual movement," as he recognized in 1866, "begun just a hundred years ago with the publication of Percy's Reliques." In time he became a valued friend to Carlyle, Morris, Rossetti, Burne-Jones, and especially Ruskin. A lifelong student of architecture, which he considered of all arts "the most quickly responsive to the instincts and desires of a people," he published his *Historical Studies of Church-Building in the Middle Ages* in 1880: his admiration for the great cathedrals of the Middle Ages was so pronounced that students could imagine him entering heaven, shading his eyes, and murmuring, "Oh, oh, oh. So overdone! So garish! So—Renaissance!" But Norton's reputation rests most on his devotion to the works of Dante: he published his translation of the *Vita Nuova* in part in 1859, then in 1867 in its entirety to accompany the Longfellow's version of the *Divine Comedy*, and his own influential prose version of the *Comedy* was issued between 1891 and 1892. His classes on Dante at Harvard, initiated in the 1870s, were legendary—reading Dante with Norton, a student remembered, "was almost an act of worship"—and led to the foundation of the Dante Society of America. Part of Norton's genius was his willingness to sally into the public sphere: in 1894 he lectured on Dante to overflow crowds, first in Baltimore and then in Cambridge, and in 1896 he contributed a substantial essay on the poet to Charles Dudley Warner's multi-volume *Library of the World's Best Literature*, thus infiltrating not simply the public libraries but the domestic interiors of a generation.

For Norton's confidence in the value of medieval studies—and more particularly the study of Dante, in whom for Norton "the mediaeval spirit found its highest and completest expression"—had ultimately very little of the ivory tower about it. Instead, he believed wholeheartedly that a humanistic education was crucial for the welfare of a democratic people. A few scholars, still laboring under the dismissive "Norton legend" perpetrated by George Santayana and Van Wyck Brooks, have attempted to characterize Norton's medievalism as a timorous antimodernism, nostalgic for the age of faith: but in fact Norton never considered the medieval Church as anything but repressive, and he charged his contemporary Mary Baker Eddy with resuscitating "medievalism in its least attractive aspect." Instead, Norton saw himself in the vanguard of a new and invigorating dispensation, the attainment of an independent conscience and a secularized social responsibility: "that union in mutual charity, confidence, and help," as he expressed it in 1867, "for common labor in the endless work to advance mankind in virtue and happiness." To this end he constructed an inspirational vision of the high Middle Ages as a period of exhilarating vitality, of psychic and communal health. This was sketched first in his early *Notes of Travel and Study in Italy* (1859); it was advanced with confidence even in lectures during the Civil War, when he portrayed the thirteenth century with its presumptive independence, individualism, and freedom of inquiry as a radiant model for the nation's rebuilding at war's end.

The mind requires mighty examples. As he had cast the thirteenth century as "a period rich in great deeds," Norton similarly projected Dante as a recognizable forebear, shaped undeniably by the doctrines of the Church yet emerging heroically, as Norton believed himself to have done, from their stultifying dominance: though the inheritor of "all the dogmatic teaching of the Roman Church," the great Florentine had taken "the material conceptions which the Church afforded to her children, and clothed upon them his own spiritual imaginations. He reverently received the husks of a false creed, and changed them by the miracle of faith into the pure wheat of truth. . . . The first heaven and the first earth passed away, and he saw a new heaven and a new earth."

Norton's installation of Dante as harbinger of a new age may strike us now as quixotic. Yet it testifies to Norton's unshakable belief in what a later generation would characterize as "relevance," the unity between academic investigation and present concerns. "History then is no record of a dead past," he insisted, "and the work of History is not so much in the exhibition to us of the chronological succession of events, or in its setting forth of direct examples for our instruction, as in its opening to us the meaning and relation of the principles by which the conduct of nations and individuals is controlled, and still more in its enlarging our souls." In sentiments like these he falls in step with the procession of noble scholars whom we seek to join and delight to honor: for, as Bill Calin once memorably observed, "The true *aristoi* are kindred spirits who give the lie to barbarism and pass along the torch of civilization."

Bibliography

Dowling, Linda. *Charles Eliot Norton: The Art of Reform in Nineteenth-Century America*. Durham, NC: U of New Hampshire P, 2007.

Turner, James. *The Liberal Education of Charles Eliot Norton*. Baltimore, MD: Johns Hopkins UP, 1999.

Workman, Leslie J. "'My First Real Tutor': John Ruskin and Charles Eliot Norton." *New England Quarterly* 62.4 (Dec. 1989): 572-86.

Tom Phillips' Dante

Karl Fugelso

On those all-too-numerous occasions when I'm forced to admit that my career revolves around pictures of a 700-year-old poem, namely the *Divine Comedy*, I'm often asked whether I've seen Tom Phillips' 138 illustrations of the *Inferno*. I usually reply that indeed I have, that I have, in fact, published some thoughts on them, and that I hope to write much more about them, as the very frequency of that question suggests their importance to Dante studies in particular and to medievalism in general.

Since 1983, when Phillips' own Talfourd Press began to print the illustrations in a *livre d'artiste* that includes his translation of the *Inferno* and initially retailed for £10,000, and particularly since 1985, when Thames and Hudson reissued the illustrations and translation in a $39.95 mass-market hardback, not many, if any, other *Commedia* images have gained wider currency. Indeed, no fewer than four copies of the Thames and Hudson edition are currently for sale at my local used-book store; many more are available on the Internet; and at least one has come to the attention of my plumber, my accountant, and a woman I met in a Firestone waiting room.

Yet, at least in the eyes of my interrogators, the illustrations are not so famous as to preclude the possibility that a specialist might have overlooked them. Nor are they apparently thought to be so banal as to be beneath scholarly consideration. In fact, judging from the curiously scant writings about them and from my conversations with many of Phillips' fans inside and outside of academia, they are seen as particularly insightful and innovative.

Though many of the illustrations comprise traditional methods and media, and though they all evince extensive academic training, they don't lack for originality in the manner with which they blend those materials, and they sometimes introduce substances rarely seen within the walls of the

Establishment. For example, according to Phillips' commentary at the end of the 1985 edition, the spatters of mud that Virgil feeds Cerberus in the second illustration of Canto 6 were created by "dropping bombs of cotton wool soaked in sugar water on to a prepared etching plate and [printing them] by the sugarlift process." And for the first illustration of the traitors in Canto 32, Phillips used "a crumpled Chinese take-away container [. . .] to simulate in the etching's soft ground the cracking of the ice in which the heads down here are buried."

Moreover, Phillips integrates those innovative media and methods with iconography that has been seen by many viewers as refreshingly personal yet faithful to the text. For the violent sinners in the first illustration of Canto 11, he depicts holes knocked into pieces of corrugated iron because "their resemblance to flared and rusted bullet holes" reminded him of "gangster-films seen as a child with my father, where bursts of gunfire caused such holes to appear spontaneously in doors and walls." And for Dante's walk over the traitors in the second illustration of Canto 32, he reworked a picture from an earlier suite of prints called *A Walk to the Studio*, "which catalogued in order all the stop-cock box-lids [. . .] that lay beneath my feet as I walked from my home to the studio [because] [t]hey have always represented to me a kind of *memento mori*, announcing death with their lugubrious colour and skull-like shape [. . .]."

Indeed, in an unusually tight melding of medium and message, Phillips sometimes introduces unorthodox subjects that at least simulate materials far from traditional but absolutely integral to Phillips' own journey in creating these illustrations, as when he portrays Canto 9 as a jumble of figures, letters, and numbers that in its "palimpsestic character" reflects "the style of some of my own notebooks for this project," and when he reproduces his bank statement behind the figure of a painting boy who represents the parallel between the "strange prodigality of artists"—particularly one who would risk seven years of work and materials on a book that was to be sold by his own imprint for £10,000 per copy—and "the extravagance of the lunatic spenders" in Canto 29.

Of course, these experiences are sometimes so particular to Phillips that, without his verbal commentary, viewers could hardly be expected to make the connections he describes. Yet many of the images touch on widespread contemporary experiences and timeless associations that provide avenues not only to how Phillips approached the *Commedia* but also how others can find relevance in a highly politicized, rather gossipy text that is very much of the moment it was written. Directly across from Dante's reference to Plutus' gibberish in Canto 7, Phillips stencils nineteen lines of fragments in English and Italian that are so repetitive and so incomplete as to constitute gobbledygook, as to invoke not only nonsensical speech in general but particularly the babble that many of us encounter in memos, directives, and other official texts. And directly across from a reference in Canto 19 to the misuse of papal authority, Phillips paints a grid of nine scenes that degrade from the papal arms to a skull and crossbones, before concluding with a scene of twelve metallic circles that have the words "ugh [. . .] the shepherd [. . .] crook" dribbled across them.

Phillips thereby constructs an extraordinarily layered vision that is both accessible and intriguing. Through direct imagery and relatively simple metaphors, as well as through highly traditional artistic media and methods, he opens the *Commedia* to viewers who prefer well-established modes of viewing Western art. By often blending those approaches with innovative material and comparatively indirect imagery, he welcomes audiences with more avant-garde tastes, particularly for the time these illustrations were created. And in grounding that innovation and obliquity in highly personal experiences, he provides a post-modern depth that may particularly appeal to the growing contingent of viewers, avant-garde or otherwise, who perceive every text as ultimately particular to its creator. As suggested by the number and range of my interrogators, he wraps a major medieval monument in such a beautiful, intricate, and slippery interpretation as to bridge many a generational and socio-cultural divide, as to open the *Commedia*, the Middle Ages, and medievalism to a host of new students.

Bibliography

Möller, Joachim. "Dante, englisch." In: *Dantes "Göttliche Komödie": Drucke und Illustationen aus Sechs Jahrhunderten* Ed. Lutz S. Malke. Berlin: Staatliche Museen zu Berlin; Faber & Faber, 2000. Pp. 153-82, esp. 168-80.

Phillips, Tom. *Works and Texts*. Introduction by Huston Paschal. London: Thames & Hudson, 1992.

Shortis, Lucy. "Eroding the Darkness: The Art of Tom Phillips." *Letter Arts Review* 14 (1997): 2-13.

Woods, A. "A New *Inferno*: Tom Phillips's Dante." *The Cambridge Quarterly* 18 (1989): 98-104.

Six Views of William Morris

Caroline Jewers

"Nay," said I, "I come not from heaven, but from Essex."
(*A Dream of John Ball*, 13)

A short autobiographical sketch now in the British Library preserves, in a strong imaginative hand, what Morris felt one should know about his life: he was born in 1834 in Walthamstow, and educated first at Marlborough College, then at Exeter College, Oxford, where he met Edward Burne-Jones. He studied architecture with George Street, finished his Oxford degree, met Dante Gabriel Rossetti, penned *The Defence of Guenevere* (1858), and married Jane Burden in 1859, before he "[b]egan the business of Decorator, etc. now known as Morris and Company in 1861." The latter paragraphs focus on his politics, underlining that he "always tended towards socialism," joining first the Democratic Federation (1883), then a year later the Socialist League "a body professing the doctrines of International Revolutionary Socialism." He edited its journal, *The Commonweal*, closing his outline casually: "... lecture often for the League, and attend to its business. Write in it poetry amongst other things." He thus summarizes with great modesty a life of integrity and dedication to good causes, and to the continual making of art. No one was bound more tightly to the remaking of the Middle Ages in Victorian England—yet his medievalism did not merely fuel nostalgia, but rather informed and shaped his dynamic vision of what could yet be reintegrated into a new order based on beauty and just principles—where art might conjoin with honest craft to replace the soulless toil of an ugly industrialized world that lacked aspiration towards higher human ideals.

A notebook from some time after 1861 shows Morris making drawings, measurements, and notes: it is like looking at Villard de Honnecourt's sketchbook. Here we find studies of armor, drawings from churches, helmets, angels, saints, tapestry designs, tile layouts, borders, birds, croziers, crowns and designs of leaves of flowers—and at the center of this thoughtful profusion, the draft of a business letter to accompany the firm's prospectus, assuring clients of their ability to handle any commission for church or house, from tiles and furniture to tapestry, stained glass, wallpaper, and glassware. Morris's Middle Ages are imaginative, tactile, organic, and holistic: he was steeped in their beauty and poetry, and in his refashioning, was directly inspired by line, meter, pattern, text, and shape. He came to the spirit of the age through his practical understanding of form and function, his direct engagement as an artisan with the processes by which objects were made, and the resulting sense of the aesthetics that produced them. For Morris, medieval craftsmen and their guilds inhabited a society where, even under feudalism, the differences between classes were "more arbitrary than real" and when the "the unit of labour was an intelligent man." He said: "It was this system, which had not learned the lesson that man was made for commerce, but supposed in its simplicity that commerce was made for man, which produced the art of the Middle Ages, wherein the harmonious co-operation of free intelligence was carried to the furthest point which has yet been attained, and which alone of all art can claim to be called Free."

An extant photograph shows the interior of Morris's study at Kelmscott House, Hammersmith. It is filled with rare books, a simple sturdy worktable covered with open illuminated manuscripts, real leaves and flowers among the folios, an ornate pen-and-ink border on a frame (with additional inks, brushes, pens, and vellum at the ready) intended for his beloved Kelmscott Press, wallpaper, chairs, tile, and furnishing fabric designed by the firm, and a print of Botticelli's *Primavera* on the wall. Joining past to present, it reveals a man without pretension fully engaged in mind and hand with his work.

A set of desk diaries from the early 1880s reveals the extent of his seamless multi-tasking: on the same day, he might weave, dye, design carpets, translate a page or two, write poetry or a lecture (on subjects as diverse as politics, art, textile fabrics and the external coverings of roofs), spend a little time in his garden, and attend the Radical Union or Society for the Protection of Ancient Buildings (affectionately known as "Anti-scrape," as he and his friends railed against the thoughtless over-restoration of ancient buildings, feeling they were better unmolested). His multi-faceted medievalism was practiced daily, and with discipline. Morris was unique as a poet, *romancier,* artist, businessman, craftsman, embroiderer and tapestry-maker, typographer, designer, colorist, translator, calligrapher, weaver, and radical. He was also a traveler, delighting in Bruges for painting, Northern France for its Gothic churches and cathedrals, Iceland for wildness, sagas, and ponies, and excursions up the Thames and into the English countryside for simple pleasures; he was exceedingly well-read, an avid manuscript collector with an expert eye, and a dedicated friend and family man, though his intimate relationships proved a source of discord as well as harmony. In his enterprises he sought to create community, and made a point of involving his inner circle with his burgeoning business and expanding creative projects. For him, each area of activity was interwoven, text with textile, manuscript with book, word with image. He considered essential the creation of beautiful books and houses, both imagined down to the smallest detail, and among makers of the Middle Ages, he made more and better than most.

A walk deep in Epping Forest among the ancient trees brings us closer to Morris the ecologist. His organic vision of abundant, ordered nature, expressed as foliate and animate, is complex, ornate, and full of interlacing, perpetual symmetry. One of his best-known paper patterns, "Acanthus" (1874-75), typifies the layering of color, and strong sense of design he brought to his work. Its sinuous green leaves are still printed today, using the same blocks, color recipes, and techniques. His flowering gardens, blending nature with the flowers he admired in manuscript illumination, are similarly still in bloom.

An acquaintance with his writings makes one marvel anew that Morris was as important as a writer and poet as he was a maker of other things: he translated *The Odyssey, The Aeneid, L'Ordene de Chevalerie* and three Old French romances (including *Amis and Amile*), and in collaboration the *Heimskringla, Beowulf,* the *Grettis Saga, Songs from the Elder Edda,* and the *Völsung Saga.* Imbued with melancholy, chivalry, and *amour de loin,* his poetry from the earliest days sought to reproduce the cadences and ornament of medieval texts, and his prose continues a similar palette of strong tones and colors. His romances, novels, plays, sketches, songs, and lectures astonish with their diversity and abundance. He admired Caxton and early printers: for the Kelmscott Press he designed three fonts (Golden, Troy, and Chaucer) and printed on vellum (for the first few special copies) and then on hand-made paper with special inks. In limited editions, he published his own works and a list that placed side-by-side Ruskin, Tennyson, and *Reynard the Fox,* Chaucer, Swinburne, *The History of Godefroy of Boloyne,* Rossetti, and *The Golden Legend.*

An appreciation of the range of his works leaves an indelible impression of the integrity of the man who was wise enough to look back into the medieval world in order to see a better present, and a way forward.

W.illiam Morris, visionary/socialist
C.reative genius
C.raftsman, art/isan

Bibliography

Banham, Joanna, and Jennifer Harris. *William Morris and the Middle Ages: A Collection of Essays, Together with a Catalogue of Works Exhibited at the Whitworth Art Gallery, 28 September – 8 December 1984.* Manchester: Manchester UP 1984.

LeMire, Eugene D. *A Bibliography of William Morris.* New Castle, DE: Oak Knoll P; London: British Library, 2006.

MacCarthy, Fiona. *William Morris.* London: Faber & Faber, 1994.

Morris, William. Manuscript resources at the British Library:

Autobiographical sketch, Ashley A1230 (vol. III, fol.172); Kelmscott House photograph, BL Add. 54316-7, item number 188; notebook, Add.45336; desk diaries, MS Add. 45407B -45411.

---. *The Defence of Guenevere*. Hammersmith, Middlesex: The Kelmscott P, 1892.

---. *Art, Labour and Socialism: With a Modern Assessment*. London: Socialist Party of Great Britain, 1967.

Parry, Linda, ed. *William Morris and the Art of Kelmscott*. Woodbridge, Suffolk: Boydell & Brewer, 1996. Occasional Papers of the Society of Antiquaries, London, 18.

Thompson, E.P. *Romantic to Revolutionary*. Stanford: Stanford UP, 1955; reissued 1988.

Victoria and Albert Museum, CIRC. 297-1955, William Morris, "Acanthus." See the wallpaper printed: http://www.vam.ac.uk/collections/paintings/videos/wallpaper/modem.html. Accessed 24 January 2011.

Contributors

Barbara K. Altman, University of Oregon
Pam Clements, Siena College
Elizabeth Emery, Montclair State University
Karl Fugelso, Towson University
Caroline Jewers, University of Kansas
Alicia C. Montoya, University of Groningen
Gwendolyn A. Morgan, Montana State University
E.L. Risden, St. Norbert College
Nils Holger Petersen, University of Copenhagen
William D. Paden, Northwestern University
F. Regina Psaki, University of Oregon
Carol L. Robinson, Kent State University - Trumbull
Roy Rosenstein, American University of Paris
Tom Shippey, St. Louis University
Jesse G. Swan, University of Northern Iowa
M.J. Toswell, University of Western Ontario
Richard Utz, Western Michigan University
Kathleen Verduin, Hope College
Veronica Ortenberg West-Harling, Oxford University
Gayle Zachmann, University of Florida

www.ingramcontent.com/pod-product-compliance
Ingram Content Group UK Ltd.
Pitfield, Milton Keynes, MK11 3LW, UK
UKHW041928190726
13854UKWH00004B/1510